# Retaining Top Employees

## Other titles in the Briefcase Books series include:

*Customer Relationship Management*
by Kristin Anderson and Carol Kerr

*Communicating Effectively* by Lani Arredondo

*Performance Management* by Robert Bacal

*Recognizing and Rewarding Employees* by R. Brayton Bowen

*Six Sigma for Managers* by Greg Brue

*Motivating Employees* by Anne Bruce and James S. Pepitone

*Leadership Skills for Managers* by Marlene Caroselli

*Negotiation Skills for Managers* by Steven Cohen

*Effective Coaching* by Marshall J. Cook

*Conflict Resolution* by Daniel Dana

*Project Management* by Gary R. Heerkens

*Managing Teams* by Lawrence Holpp

*Hiring Great People* by Kevin C. Klinvex,
Matthew S. O'Connell, and Christopher P. Klinvex

*Empowering Employees* by Kenneth L. Murrell and Mimi
Meredith

*Presentation Skills for Managers*, by Jennifer Rotondo
and Mike Rotondo

*The Manager's Guide to Business Writing*
by Suzanne D. Sparks

*Skills for New Managers* by Morey Stettner

*Manager's Survival Guide* by Morey Stettner

*Interviewing Skills for Managers* by Carolyn B. Thompson

*Managing Multiple Projects* by Michael Tobis and Irene Tobis

---

To learn more about titles in the Briefcase Books series go to
**www.briefcasebooks.com**

You'll find the tables of contents, downloadable sample chapters, information on the authors, discussion guides for using these books in training programs, and more.

A
Briefcase
Book

# Retaining Top Employees

## J. Leslie McKeown

**McGraw-Hill**

New York  Chicago  San Francisco  Lisbon  London
Madrid  Mexico City  Milan  New Delhi  San Juan
Seoul  Singapore  Sydney  Toronto

# McGraw-Hill

*A Division of The* **McGraw·Hill** *Companies*

Copyright © 2002 by The McGraw-Hill Companies, Inc. All rights reserved.
Printed in the United States of America. Except as permitted under the
United States Copyright Act of 1976, no part of this publication may be
reproduced or distributed in any form or by any means, or stored in a database or retrieval system, without the prior written permission of the publisher.

1 2 3 4 5 6 7 8 9 0 AGM/AGM 0 9 8 7 6 5 4 3 2

ISBN 0-07-138756-0

Library of Congress Cataloging-in-Publication Data applied for.

*This is a* CWL Publishing Enterprises Book, *developed and produced for*
*McGraw-Hill by* CWL Publishing Enterprises, *John A. Woods, President. For*
*more information, contact CWL Publishing Enterprises, 3010 Irvington Way,*
*Madison, WI 53713-3414, www.cwlpub.com. Robert Magnan served as editor.*
*For McGraw-Hill, the sponsoring editor is Catherine Dassopoulos, and the*
*publisher is Jeffrey Krames.*

*Printed and bound by Quebecor World Martinsburg.*

This publication is designed to provide accurate and authoritative information in regard to the subject matter covered. It is sold with the understanding
that neither the author nor the publisher is engaged in rendering legal,
accounting, or other professional service. If legal advice or other expert
assistance is required, the services of a competent professional person
should be sought.
> —*From a Declaration of Principles jointly adopted by a Committee*
> *of the American Bar Association and a Committee of Publishers*

McGraw-Hill books are available at special quantity discounts to use as pre-
miums and sales promotions, or for use in corporate training programs. For
more information, please write to the Director of Special Sales, McGraw-Hill,
2 Penn Plaza, New York, NY 10128. Or contact your local bookstore.

 This book is printed on recycled, acid-free paper containing a minimum of 50% recycled de-inked fiber.

# Contents

114055

# Preface

High-performing employees are great people to have around. They hit targets, add value, contribute to the organization overall, and inspire others.

For those same reasons, your top employees are also those most likely to be pursued or at least actively welcomed by other organizations.

Top performers also tend to have an inconveniently realistic idea of their own worth and an uncanny knack of knowing what other career options are available to them at any time.

They can also (sometimes) be cranky, independent-minded mavericks who can be distinctly hard to manage.

All of this taken together makes the manager's job of retaining the best employees a delicate amalgam of motivation, support, diplomatic chastising, and inspiration.

Between providing resources and setting challenges, agreeing to compensation and coaching for higher performance, rewarding achievement and encouraging teamwork, the top performer's manager is increasingly expected to be some sort of corporate Superman or Wonder Woman.

While this book won't turn you into a superhero, it will provide you with the tips, tools, and techniques you need to not only manage your key employees, but also inspire, motivate, and—above all—*keep* them.

I've personally been benefiting from, managing, developing, challenging, retaining (and occasionally firing) key employees in organizations large and small, for-profit and not-for-profit, for over 20 years. The lessons I've learned (sometimes painfully) from many cultures and countries are in this book. I know you will benefit from them.

## Special Features

The idea behind the books in the Briefcase Series is to give you
practical information written in a friendly person-to-person style.
The chapters are short, deal with tactical issues, and include
lots of examples. They also feature numerous sidebars designed
to give you different types of specific information. Here's a
description of these sidebars and how they're used in this book.

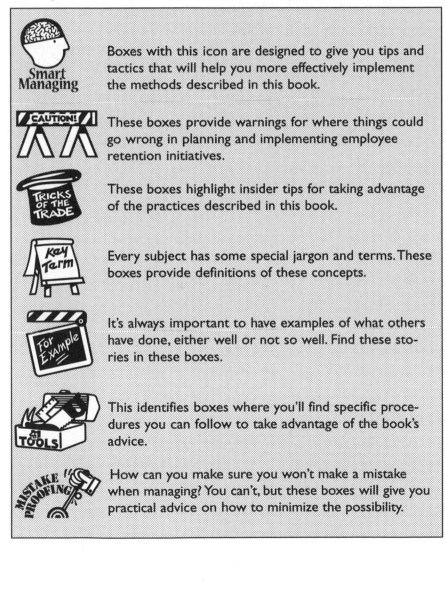

**Smart Managing**
Boxes with this icon are designed to give you tips and
tactics that will help you more effectively implement
the methods described in this book.

**CAUTION!**
These boxes provide warnings for where things could
go wrong in planning and implementing employee
retention initiatives.

**TRICKS OF THE TRADE**
These boxes highlight insider tips for taking advantage
of the practices described in this book.

**Key Term**
Every subject has some special jargon and terms. These
boxes provide definitions of these concepts.

**For Example**
It's always important to have examples of what others
have done, either well or not so well. Find these stories in these boxes.

**TOOLS**
This identifies boxes where you'll find specific procedures you can follow to take advantage of the book's
advice.

**MISTAKE PROOFING**
How can you make sure you won't make a mistake
when managing? You can't, but these boxes will give you
practical advice on how to minimize the possibility.

## Acknowledgments

Most of all, I owe a debt greater than an acknowledgement to my partner in this book (and in all things), Julie Wilson. As well as managing our business, Julie is responsible for motivating, chastising, and inspiring me, every day. She does an incredible job and is the only real superhero I've met.

I am indebted to Hank Karp and Danilo Sirias, whose foundational and insightful paper "Retaining Generation X" has influenced my thinking for some time now and the structure of which is used (with their permission) in Chapter 4. You can read more from Hank and Danilo in their latest book, *Bridging the Boomer-Xer Gap: Creating Authentic Teams for High Performance at Work* (Consulting Psychologists Press, Inc., 2002).

Finally, my thanks also to John Woods and Robert Magnan at CWL Publishing Enterprises, who are responsible for the original idea and for lifting the manuscript to the level of excellence required for inclusion in this series. For Bob in particular, my thanks for wrangling the first draft into manageable size.

Of course, any errors of fact or interpretation are entirely my own.

# "Employee What?!"

*Along the journey we commonly forget its goal. ...*
*Forgetting our objectives is the most frequent stupidity in*
*which we indulge ourselves.*
                                        —Friedrich Nietzsche

*A journey is like marriage. The certain way to be wrong*
*is to think you control it.*
                                        —John Steinbeck

In this introductory chapter, we will:

- Look at exactly what "employee retention" is.
- Explore where the concept first came from.
- See how it has developed over recent years.
- Examine three trends that are currently shaping employee retention strategies.

## Just What Is "Employee Retention" Anyway?

There is no secret code or formula that precisely defines "employee retention." Ask 10 managers what they mean by the term and you'll receive 10 (sometimes very) different answers. Answers like these:

- "Employee retention? You mean stopping people from leaving this organization?"
- "Employee retention is all about keeping good people."
- "Getting our compensation and benefits into line with the marketplace."
- "Stock options, crèche facilities, and other perks."
- "It's got to do with our culture and how we treat people."
- "Staunching the high employee turnover we have in department x or job function y."
- "Presenting a consistent, effective employer proposition across the entire employee life cycle, thus ensuring we source, hire, manage, and develop employees who partner with us in achieving our organizational goals."

As you can see, managers' perceptions of the meaning of employee retention can vary from the mechanical ("Reduce this employee turnover figure to an acceptable level") to the abstract ("It's about our culture and values"). Definitions can be couched in curt, wholly objective phrases or in flowery, vague "corporate speak." Some managers view employee retention as a distinct, controllable element of labor management ("It's a matter of compensation and benefits") and others consider it a cross-functional, pervasive, and seemingly all-encompassing set of values or methodologies ("It's about our culture and how we treat people").

Which of all these "flavors and colors" of employee retention is right?

Is employee retention any single one of the definitions cited above? Is it a specific combination of two or more of those definitions? Is it something else entirely that we haven't mentioned?

Well, the answer to all those questions is ... "Yes."

Employee retention is each of the definitions cited above. It can also be a specific combination of two or more of those definitions. And it is some other things that we haven't even mentioned yet.

How can this be? How can one seemingly straightforward concept be so many disparate, sometimes contradictory things?

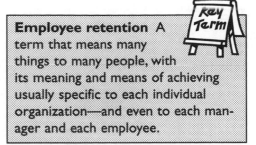

**Employee retention** A term that means many things to many people, with its meaning and means of achieving usually specific to each individual organization—and even to each manager and each employee.

The answer is because employee retention—effective employee retention—is not some externally generated set of activities or metrics that have a life of their own and that are applicable to every circumstance. As we will see throughout this book, effective employee retention is something that is very specific to each individual organization.

Two organizations in the same industry, making the same product, in the same town, with the same labor pool and the same customers and the same suppliers can see employee retention very differently, because of differing management styles and different past experiences. Even within the same organization, employee retention can mean something entirely different from one division to another or from one manager to another. And within any one division, under any one manager, what's key to keeping one employee may not be relevant to another.

### Biotech vs. Burger Bar

What employee retention means to the biotech company down the road, peopled with chemists and concerned with R&D issues, is very different from what it means to the burger chain franchise in the next street, employing students and facing speed-of-production issues. And the way each company addresses it is necessarily different as well.

The biotech company may think of employee retention primarily in relation to a handful of key chemists whom they want to retain for a period of years, while a product moves through its R&D cycle, through testing and certification, and finally into marketing and sales. In contrast, the burger joint is likely to be concerned about retention problems across a much broader category of employees and with a time horizon of months rather than years.

> **⚠️ CAUTION!**
>
> **"No Generalization Is Worth a Damn ..."**
>
> "No generalization is worth a damn, including this one!" Those words of caution—attributed to Mark Twain, George Bernard Shaw, and Oliver Wendell Holmes—seem particularly appropriate here. All the generalizations about employee retention, no matter how wise, are worth little if you don't apply them judiciously.
>
> Every organization—and every department or division in every organization—is a different environment for employee retention. Additionally, within each organization, department, and division, circumstances will change from year to year, month to month, maybe even from day to day, in such a way as to render your carefully constructed employee retention goals, strategies, and tactics either obsolete or at least in need of a good overhaul. If you know your environment and keep alert to changes, you can make the most of any generalizations about employee retention.

So you will not find in this book (or elsewhere) one prescriptive, generic answer to the question of employee retention, no single plan that fits every situation. Instead, you will discover how to define employee retention for yourself, for your organization, and even for specific departments or divisions in your organization. You will learn how to establish realistic, organization-specific employee retention goals, how to select the right strategies and tactics to attain those goals, and how to gauge the success of those strategies and tactics. Finally, and most importantly, you'll learn how to monitor and vary your employee retention goals, strategies, and tactics over time, as your organization's circumstances change.

## What "Employee Retention" Used to Mean

Let's start by getting our definitions and vocabulary right. This entails understanding just a little history.

The term "employee retention" first began to appear with regularity on the business scene in the 1970s and early '80s. Until then, during the early and mid-1900s, the essence of the relationship between employer and employee had been (by and large) a statement of the status quo:

You come work for me, do a good job, and, so long as economic conditions allow, I will continue to employ you.

It was not unusual for people who entered the job market as late as the 1950s and '60s to remain with one employer for a very long time—sometimes for the duration of their working life. If they changed jobs, it was usually a major career and life decision, and someone who made many and frequent job changes was seen as somewhat out of the ordinary.

As a natural result of this "status quo" employer-employee relationship, an employee leaving his or her job voluntarily was seen as an aberration, something that shouldn't really have happened. After all, the essence of "status quo" is just that little or nothing should change in the relationship—and leaving was a pretty big change!

So, in the 1970s and later, as job mobility and voluntary job changes began to increase dramatically, the "status quo" model began to fray substantially at the edges. Employers found themselves with a new phenomenon to consider: employee turnover.

## The Rise of Employee Retention as a Management Tool

As organizations began to feel the impact of the rise of voluntary employee turnover, so a matching management tool began to be developed—employee retention.

In this earliest, simplest form, employee retention was the

**Employee turnover** Percentage of the workforce who left the organization in any particular period. If, for example, an organization employed an average of 100 people during one particular year and 45 of them left (for any reason) during that year, the theoretical employee turnover rate for that year would be 45%.

In practice, managers are mostly concerned in gauging the rate of *voluntary departures*—employees who choose to leave of their own free will. People may leave the organization for many other reasons—retirement, ill health, firing, or enforced redundancy. These "involuntary separations" are usually excluded from the calculation of the employee turnover rate, thus allowing the organization to concentrate on the controllable reasons for employees leaving.

## Understand the Reasons for Job Mobility

**Smart Managing**    The increase in voluntary employee turnover is in large part the result of an increase in job mobility—in essence a reduction of the friction involved in switching jobs—and is caused by a number of factors coming together, primarily:

• More information about job openings elsewhere, through TV, radio, newspapers, magazines, and the Web.
• Dramatic reductions in the cost of travel and relocation.
• A shift in personal values as the global economy moved out of post-war austerity.
• An increase in skills development opportunities and cross-training, making people more "employable."
• The decline of the industrial conglomerate, breaking up old hiring practices.
• The globalization of manufacturing competition, requiring more mobility of skills.
• Large-scale layoffs, reducing the loyalty employees felt toward their employers.
• The rise of small and medium-sized businesses as competitive employers, providing viable employment opportunities in most urban areas.

aspirin for the headache—a straightforward response to the rise in employee turnover: how can we stop people voluntarily leaving this organization at the rate they are doing?

However, as we've already seen, the root cause of voluntary employee turnover—increased job mobility—was a complex amalgam of trends and events (see sidebar on mobility), not any single, simple thing.

Because of the complexity of the changes happening in the industrial and commercial environment, it took some time for employers to understand that, in essence, the power in the employer-employee relationship was shifting from the employer to the employee.

Eventually, it became clear that trying to maintain the old, paternalistic "status quo" employer-employee relationship was not going to reduce the growing rate of employee turnover from which many organizations were suffering. Employers had to do something to staunch the flow.

## Tweaking Around the Edges

The first steps in employee retention were simply to perform an iteration on the old employer-employee relationship—nothing too dramatic, just some attempts to make the existing relationship better, more palatable for the employee. Employers (understandably) wanted to begin with those things that met the following three criteria:

- Familiar ground in the old employer-employee relationship
- Easy to track in terms of employee turnover cause and effect
- Readily quantifiable

First attempts at employee retention, therefore, dealt primarily with *hygiene factors*—compensation, benefits, and the physical aspects of the working environment (for example, employee health and safety, toilet breaks, shift planning and duration, etc.), all of which fulfilled the three criteria above.

Many organizations began to pull their compensation packages more into line with something called the "market level." (With the increasingly free flow of information, it was becoming more and more difficult for employers to pay an employee dramatically less than a competitor, so this wasn't much of a concession.) It became more common for organizations to include nonmonetary "hygiene factors" such as workplace health, safety, and comfort in the basic deal they offered to employees.

> **Key Term**
>
> **Hygiene factors** Items that do not in themselves motivate employees, but that are necessary to prevent dissatisfaction. The term comes from Frederick Herzberg, one of the most influential management teachers and consultants of the postwar era. Herzberg studied employees in the 1950s and 1960s and found that certain factors tended to cause employees to feel unsatisfied with their job. That research led him to develop his "hygiene theory." Among the hygiene factors (also known as *satisfiers*) Herzberg identified were physical work environment, company policies, and salary.

## What "Employee Retention" Means Now

By the time we reached the late '80s, organizations had made most of the one-time realignments of compensation and benefits possible. Although the issue of compensation and benefits would continue to form part of every organization's employee retention toolkit, there was a growing realization—on the part of both employers and employees—that there was more to employee retention than hygiene factors.

Most important to the development of the now fully fledged employee retention industry was the realization that if employee retention was to be effective and sustainable—if it was to work in the long run and not just produce a single, temporary dip in employee turnover—there was a need for a holistic approach to the individual employee that would go beyond simply adjusting the employee's compensation and benefits.

### Meeting "Higher" Needs

What came into play was something called Maslow's hierarchy of needs—a well-accepted concept that began in psychology, spread to other areas of life, and then slowly began to make a profound impact on working life and, in particular, on the understanding of what employee retention really means.

Abraham Maslow was a psychologist who focused on

---

**Competitive Compensation Is Just the Entry Fee**

**Smart Managing**    As we'll see over and over again in this book, it's impossible to build a sustainable, effective employee retention strategy on the basis of competitive compensation and benefits alone. (We discuss the role of compensation and benefits in effective employee retention later in this chapter and in detail in Chapter 5.) Ensuring that your compensation and benefits are competitive is just the entry fee to playing the "employee retention strategy game."

In other words, if your compensation and benefits aren't competitive, you've got to fix them before you start thinking seriously about serious, effective employee retention. However, making your compensation and benefits competitive only brings you to the starting gate—it's what you do after that point that makes all the difference.

human potential, believing that we all strive to reach the highest levels of our capabilities. He is considered the founder of humanistic psychology. In his book *Motivation and Personality* (1954), he introduced psychological concepts that are now standard, such as "needs hierarchy," "self-actualization," and "peak experience."

Maslow once summarized his findings as follows: "The unhappiness, unease and unrest in the world today is caused by people living far below their capacity." Substitute "workplace" for "world" and you can see the impact his thinking has on employee retention.

Maslow created a model of human needs that's often depicted in the form of a pyramid. The foundation level consists of basic biological or physiological needs—oxygen, water, food, and so forth: these needs are the strongest because we need to satisfy them to remain alive. Our needs in the next level up are for safety and security. One level higher are social needs—a sense of belonging, acceptance, friendship, love. Above that level are ego needs: the need for respect, esteem, recognition, and status. Finally, we have the peak—self-actualization, fulfillment, self-development. Maslow showed that we must satisfy our needs one level at a time, going from basic to self-actualization.

The implications for employee retention were enormous and wide-ranging. Just looking at the terms in the paragraph above provides a shopping list of ways in which organizations have been trying to achieve employee retention during the past 10 to 15 years:

> **Key Term**
>
> **Maslow's hierarchy of needs** A model of human needs, from basic biological and physiological needs to self-actualization. We must satisfy our needs one level at a time, going from basic to self-actualization.

- Acceptance (assimilation programs, orientation programs, company retreats)
- Respect (suggestion programs, diversity programs, 360-degree evaluations, corporate visions and values)
- Status (job titles, executive perks, cars, corner offices,

delegated authority)

- Recognition (promotion, fast-track programs, employee of the month programs, award programs)
- Fulfillment and self-development (lifelong learning programs, funded education programs, sabbaticals)

## Don't Grow Employee Retention Weeds!

When you understand that effective employee retention goes beyond simply adjusting compensation and benefits, you can avoid the most common, costly, and least effective approach to employee retention—the "employee retention weed garden." This is the syndrome of trying to improve employee retention, only to find that the problem comes back worse than before. Here are the basic steps:

1. An organization recognizes that it has an employee turnover problem.
2. The organization sets up a task force, does some benchmarking, and revises its compensation and benefits packages (rightly addressing the lowest, most basic level of the employees' hierarchy of needs).
3. The organization sees a temporary (12- to 24-month) reduction in its employee turnover problem.
4. Employees, now that their basic needs are being met, naturally begin to seek fulfillment of their higher needs—acceptance, esteem, fulfillment, and self-development. The demand increases for interesting projects, meaningful relationships with managers and colleagues, and a clear career path.
5. Faced with such demands, the senior managers feel that their employees, whose compensation and benefits have just been substantially improved, should be grateful and happily and productively engaged in their assigned tasks and not militating for yet more perks.
6. Embittered, the senior managers vow to "never be trapped by this employee retention malarkey again." Employees will be paid appropriate to the job and that's it. Conceding on

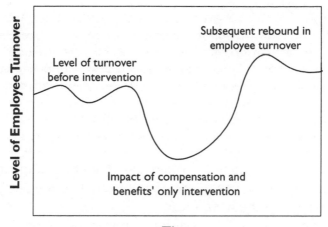

**Time**

Figure 1-1. The employee retention "weed garden"

anything else obviously brings only trouble and grief.

7. The employees become increasingly aware that the senior managers are withdrawing from constructive engagement and acting surly toward any suggestions from the employees.
8. The organizational culture spirals downward into mutual distrust and the employee turnover problem returns—only, like weeds in a garden, even harder to eradicate.

Figure 1-1 depicts the "employee retention 'weed garden.'"

In the chapters that follow, we'll see what those higher, "non-compensation-and-benefits" needs are, how they are met, and how to plan and implement an employee retention strategy that incorporates ways to meet them.

## What "Employee Retention" Might Mean Soon

We've seen that employee retention started as a simplistic, "compensation and benefits" response to the systemic rise in voluntary employee turnover, then developed into a wider, holistic approach, addressing deeper needs such as acceptance, esteem, and self-actualization.

Before we move into the next section (and begin developing your specific response to employee retention issues), let's close

> ### Plan to Address Higher Needs
> In designing your employee retention strategy, recognize in advance that compensation and benefits are just a start (as we'll cover in Chapter 5), so you can begin dealing with the other, higher needs of your employees. By anticipating those higher needs and planning in advance to meet them—once you've addressed the basic, monetary needs—you and your fellow managers will not be surprised when your employees begin that dialogue. In fact, you'll be prepared for it.

this section by looking at the main trends that are impacting approaches to employee retention currently and are likely to do so increasingly in the near future.

In particular, we will look at four prominent factors in current thinking on employee retention:

- Core competencies and outsourcing
- The rise of the "free agent"
- The so-called "war for talent"
- Becoming an employer of choice

### Core Competencies and Outsourcing

In 1990 C.K. Prahalad and Gary Hamel wrote an article titled "The Core Competence of the Corporation" (*Harvard Business Review*, May-June 1990). Their idea—that organizations had *core competencies* (skills and activities that are essential to an organization's success and that the organization must do well) and not-so-core competencies (skills and activities that are not essential to an organization's success and that it probably isn't doing well)—slowly gained acceptance as a competitive strategy. As a result, the book that Prahalad and Hamel pub-

> **Key Term**
> **Core competence** (or **competency**) "A bundle of skills and technologies that enables a company to provide a particular benefit to customers." That's how C.K. Prahalad and Gary Hamel define this term in *Competing for the Future*. Core competencies contribute to the competitiveness of a range of products or services. They transcend any particular product or service and perhaps any particular business unit within the organization.

---

### Dump or Outsource

MegaOffex, an office equipment manufacturer, might conclude that its core competencies are in designing, manufacturing, and marketing office equipment and not in manufacturing and selling office supplies. It would either dump its supplies business, thus freeing up its resources and people to concentrate on core competencies, or sell it to another organization for which manufacturing and selling office supplies is the core activity ... or to a competitor that does not follow the core competency model.

Later, MegaOffex might decide that providing catering facilities for its 23,000 employees is also not a core competency and thus decide to outsource that activity to a catering company.

---

lished several years later, *Competing for the Future* (Harvard Business School Press, 1994), has become a best seller.

The essence of the core competency model—that organizations should either dump non-core activities entirely or outsource them to other organizations (for which the activities are core)—began to make an impact on the workplace from about 1997 on.

The realization that organizations should limit their business areas had a profound impact on the development of employee retention strategy for medium-sized and larger organizations during the late '90s. In essence, it allowed them in certain circumstances to remove employee turnover as a management concern altogether.

The argument around the board table (or inside the CEO's head) goes something like this:

**Question:** We're experiencing excessive employee turnover in our plastics division. Turnover everywhere else in our company seems relatively OK. We're good employers. Why should this be?

**Response:** Manufacturing plastics isn't our core activity—we make and sell ballpoint pens. The only reason we have a plastics division is to supply the raw materials for our pens. It's no wonder the employees are unhappy and leaving. We don't know how to run a plastics manufacturing operation. Our core skills are assembling and marketing pens. We'll never know how to run a plastics manufacturing plant correctly—it's just not a strategic fit with our skills.

**Solution:** Let's sell the plastics division to somebody who's in the plastics business and then buy back the finished product from them. They'll make a better and cheaper product than we can make. And, because we won't have a plastics division, we won't have a turnover problem.

As a result of pruning and refocusing on core competencies, many larger organizations were able to remove major employee turnover issues with one stroke.

Now, many new companies, divisions, plants, product lines, and other organizational units are adopting the core competency model right at the outset, focusing on hiring employees only for their core activities and purchasing non-core products and services externally. This trend is very likely to continue in the future.

## The Rise of the "Free Agent"

During the late '90s and (only just) into the new millennium, one event (temporarily) impacted the concept of employee retention more than any other—the rise and fall of the dot-com phenomenon.

As a result of a combination of factors—primarily the easy availability of capital, the temporary suspension of the profit principle, and the invasion of the workforce by Generation X—the dot-com phenomenon caused two particular distortions in thinking about what constituted employee retention.

The first of those distortions was somewhat superficial; we can discuss and dismiss it in short order. The second distortion had a greater impact on employee retention.

During the dot-com ascension, there was an overemphasis on the perceived needs of one narrow group of employees—20- to 30-year-old professionals. This in turn produced an emphasis on those aspects of employee retention that could be purchased with money—most commonly the following, in order of perceived importance and impact:

> **Generation X**  People who were born between 1963 and 1982, some of whom are still entering the workforce for the first time
>
> At the time of writing (2002), there are two generations of workers who hold most of the jobs. The older group is the Baby Boomers (those born between 1945 and 1962). They hold the greatest share of policy-making and upper-level positions, except in some high-tech companies, some startups, and industries often identified with "youth"—entertainment, advertising, graphic design, etc. The other generation is Generation X.
>
> The designation comes from a book published in 1991 by Douglas Coupland, *Generation X: Tales for an Accelerated Culture* (St. Martin's Press), in which he defined the years as 1960-1970. In their book *13th Gen: Abort, Retry, Ignore, Fail?* (Vintage Books, 1993), Neil Howe and Bill Strauss set the Gen X years as 1961-1981. Other dates have been proposed. The years are just numbers, however, because Generation X is an attitude, a culture, and—of course—a stereotype.
>
> A major distinction between the two groups is that while Boomers seem somewhat at ease with this designation, Gen-Xers seem uniformly to bristle at being referred to as such. Use the label with care!

- stock options
- BMWs (or occasionally Porsches)
- fussball tables
- free soft drinks

Even before the dot-com boom began to bust, it was becoming clear to most people (employees and employers alike) that this was nothing more or less than a Maslow's hierarchy of needs list, adapted for modern times. The much-vaunted stock options were no more than a "hygiene" factor like any other element of "compensation and benefits" (and with less impact on employee retention, as it turned out, than a basic salary package). The fussball table and free soft drinks were simply a reincarnation of the employee cafeteria. The BMWs and Porsches were a direct substitute for ... um ... the BMWs and Porsches of old.

Later in the book, we'll examine in more detail the impact of the dot-com era and, in particular, the hugely overstated role that stock options have come to play in employee retention.

A much more important and lasting aspect of the dot-com era that will continue to materially impact many employers' approaches to employee retention is the rise of the external consultant or *free agent*.

> **Key Term** **Free agent** An independent worker. Free agents would include the self-employed, freelancers, independent contractors, people running home-based businesses or "micro businesses," solo practitioners, and independent professionals. Some studies have estimated that free agents account for one-third of the workforce.

Buoyed by a high economy, large sums of money in the system, and the enormous demand for almost every imaginable skill, many employees launched themselves into self-employment. (At the height of free agency, Daniel H. Pink in his book, *Free Agent Nation* [Warner Books, 2001], estimated—somewhat liberally—that 33 million people had adopted this status.)

Although described in many different (and often exotic) ways, free agent status is in essence the employee response to the core competency argument. The argument around the kitchen table or inside the free agent's head goes something like this:

1. If my employer can redefine its core competency at any time, I have no job security left. I can be deemed "non-core" at any time and let go. Maybe I should take my destiny into my own hands.
2. This core competency model is a good one. If organizations have core competencies, so have I. I'll find out what my core competency is and then sell it to the highest bidder.
3. Concentrating on core competencies, resizing, downsizing … whatever you call it, it all means one thing to me—I'm under even more pressure to do more in less time with fewer resources. My entire work-life balance is shot to pieces. I'll become a free agent. When I'm free from these importunate demands from my employer, I can develop a

> ### Researching "Brand You"
> If you work with a lot of free agents, or just want to know
> more about the phenomenon, check out Dan Pink's book,
> *Free Agent Nation*, Tom Peters' slim tome, *The Brand You 50: Fifty Ways to
> Transform Yourself from an "Employee" into a Brand That Shouts Distinction,
> Commitment, and Passion!* (Knopf, 1999) (an easy read—the book isn't
> much longer than the title), *Fast Company* magazine, and
> www.guru.com.
>   For other resources, fire up a search engine such as www.google.com
> and type "free agent" or "Brand You" in the search box.

proper work-life balance at home.

The first argument has much validity: it's merely an extension of the reason why people have long become consultants or self-employed—to gain more control over their future. It's an echo of one of the most basic of Maslow's hierarchy of needs—the need for security.

The second and third arguments—often combined in a concept called "Brand You" and much promoted by *Fast Company* magazine, management guru Tom Peters, and others—lured many people into becoming free agents for all the wrong reasons.

Many free agents found out the following facts of free agent life:

- Except for a few exceptional individuals, life as a free agent brings even less chance of work-life balance than the average full-time job.
- Life as a free agent is very lonely: most people are too gregarious to thrive in the socially barren world of free agency.
- Free agent status is exactly how *not* to concentrate on your core competencies. To be a free agent, you also have to be good at "non-core" activities, such as marketing and selling yourself, writing proposals and negotiating fees, bookkeeping, and typing letters.
- If you really want just to concentrate on core competencies, the best bet is that boring old concept, the full-time

job. With a full-time job, your employer handles all those other tasks and lets you concentrate on what you are good at and want to do—the very definition of core competency.

When the money began to dry up and the economy turned downward, many free agents didn't have the marketing and sales skills necessary to get enough work to pay the bills. As the dot-com era ended in late 2000 and early 2001, many people who had tried the free agent option, with varying success, gradually returned to full-time employee status.

## Free Agents and Employee Retention

The rise and fall of the free agent redefined the role of the independent worker and is impacting employee retention strategies in two (complementary) ways:

1. Employers began to see that there are many people (employees and potential employees) who are free agents at heart, by their desires, passions, and ambitions. Such people respond to different "retention stimuli" than the typical employee, who rarely, if ever, thinks about striking out alone.
2. It's now better understood and accepted that many jobs in an organization (even those that are "core") need not be "jobs" at all—they can readily be transformed into assignments that can be performed by independent contractors. This in turn radically alters the employee retention equation for those relationships.

**Free Agents Among Your Employees**

Smart managers recognize that employees and potential employees have changed over the past decade. Many of them are free agents at heart. They're motivated differently—and to keep them around you need to treat them differently. Later chapters will offer some suggestions, but it's up to you to know your employees and how they think and feel.

In Chapter 7 we'll examine in depth the impact on employee retention of hiring independent contractors—free agents—rather than, or alongside, "core employees."

## The War for Talent

After the concept of core competencies and the rise of the free agent, the third key factor in current thinking on employee retention is a theory encompassing employee acquisition (hiring), employee retention, and performance management sometimes called "the war for talent."

When this phrase was first used is lost in the dusty web pages of time, but it gained most exposure when the consulting firm of McKinsey & Company in 1997 issued a report (and later a book) titled *The War for Talent*, based on a study involving 77 companies and almost 6,000 managers and executives.

The "war for talent" mindset proposes that:

- The number of high-caliber individuals out there who can perform your organization's "mission-critical" (core competency) tasks is limited.
- Those individuals are basically mercenaries for hire.
- You're in a war with your competitors to attract and keep such individuals.

Later espoused by many prominent "HR thinkers," such as John Sullivan of San Francisco State University, the "war for talent" approach stresses that employers must present a compelling "employee value proposition"—essentially a set of reasons why a potential employee should come and work for you rather than go elsewhere.

## Where Does Retention Start?

Whatever the validity of the underlying approach, the "war for talent" methodology made an undeniably positive impact on employee retention thinking, through the realization that it's much easier and considerably less expensive to retain a current good employee than to find a new one.

That's something that sales and marketing executives have

**Retention Begins with Presence and Image**

Effective retention begins before the hire—in your recruitment literature, of course, but also in corporate and product literature, advertisements (for recruitment and for sales), press releases, product branding, company image, management reputation, and a myriad of other messages that your organization puts out into the marketplace about what it is, what it does, and how it does it.

As we'll see later, these signals act as filters in two ways: they determine the type of person who applies to work for your organization and they set the bar for later decisions by the employee about whether or not to stay with your organization and for how long.

long known about customers, that it's much cheaper and easier to keep and develop current customers than to find new ones. The "war for talent" approach emphasizes that employee retention can't just start months or years after a person joins the organization, because the employee's perceptions of the organization are massively influenced by the following aspects:

- what he or she saw and heard before joining the organization,
- how he or she was treated right at the outset of the relationship, and only then
- how he or she is treated on an ongoing basis.

In other words, starting to work on retention a year or two after a person joins the organization (a typical response in the "employee turnover = employee retention" mindset), when the possibility or probability of the employee leaving has become obvious or acute, is much too late. Even starting to work on retention as soon as a person joins the organization is still too late.

### Becoming an Employer of Choice

Finally, in our survey of current trends in employee retention, we come to the concept of "employer of choice." It's basically a variation of the "war for talent" approach.

In its raw form, the aggressive "war for talent" approach to employee retention has proved somewhat too strong for many organizations and irrelevant to many situations. In particular, the purist version of "war for talent" calls for grading employees into streams ("A," "B," and "C" performers) and taking differing approaches for each: promote "A," develop "B," and "lose"— fire—"C." This theory was an extension of the now-renowned grading system introduced to GE by Jack Welch. Although it's useful in some circumstances, this approach has proved difficult to implement and sometimes inappropriate. It's also directly opposed to the collaborative, supportive working environment that many organizations want to promote.

As a result, a hybrid version of the "war for talent" approach developed, emphasizing the benchmarking activities necessary to develop the "employee value proposition" and involving the organization in adopting the employee retention best practices of similar organizations. In this approach, known (briefly) as "best in class" and now more often referred to as "employer of choice," the organization:

- Investigates and adopts best practices in retention
- Extends retention backward to pre-hire activities (as in the earlier sidebar)
- Pushes the impact of retention forward beyond the hire to incorporate the employee's management, development, and managed separation from the organization.

You may be thinking that this whole discussion of "employer of choice" and "war for talent" is irrelevant here. After all, you're just a manager, not the CEO. What can *you* do?

You can still think in terms of the "employee value proposition" that you present to job prospects. You can still think in terms of retention beginning with your first contact with a job prospect. Finally, you can do your best to be a "manager of choice."

## Manager's Checklist for Chapter 1

❏ There is no single definition of employee retention that fits all circumstances. You'll use this book to develop the correct definition for your organization and your particular unit.

❏ The concept of employee retention developed as a response to increasing voluntary employee turnover.

❏ Initially, employee retention dealt mostly with employee "hygiene factors"—primarily compensation and benefits.

❏ It soon became clear that sustained employee retention called for a more holistic approach, that dealt with employees' "higher needs" such as acceptance, esteem, and self-fulfillment.

❏ Three particular trends are currently shaping employee retention strategies:

- The concept of "core competencies."
- The rise of the "free agent."
- The concept of becoming an "employer of choice."

# The Secret's
# in the Swing

*Golf is not a game of great shots. It is a game of the least
misses. The people who win make the least mistakes.*
—Gene Littler

In Chapter 1 we traced the history and development of the
employer-employee relationship and saw how current trends
are changing the nature of effective employee retention.

In the first part of this chapter, we take a high-level look at
four important implications arising from those changes:

1. We need to develop a "retention mindset": employee
   mobility is here to stay, and we must learn to manage it,
   not resist it.
2. No "strategy" can make people stay.
3. People stay where they feel at home.
4. Effective retention strategies focus on building a welcoming environment where people want to stay.

In the second part of this chapter, we summarize what follows in the rest of the book by outlining the five steps to build-

ing a truly effective employee retention strategy, using a golfing metaphor. (Don't worry: you don't need to understand anything about golf!)

## Develop a Retention Mindset

The changes in the old "status quo" employer-employee relationship discussed in Chapter 1 require a shift in our understanding of what constitutes effective retention. In this section we're going to examine four ways in which we must adjust our thinking to reflect those changes.

Some of the discussion in this first half is necessarily conceptual, as we build a mental picture of how to address retention. Don't worry if you cannot immediately see a concrete application of all that follows. Starting in the second half of this chapter and continuing in the chapters that follow, we'll move into the steps involved in retaining employees (specifically, your top performers) and the practical application will become clearer.

### Go with the Flow

The first implication of the changes in the employer-employee relationship is that we must change our mindset and learn to accept that job mobility is here to stay. Let me give you an example of what I mean.

My little town (Tiburon, just across the bridge from San Francisco) is at the end of a peninsula. If I want to go anywhere, I've got to brave the traffic on Highway 101—there's just no way around it.

When I moved here, at first I thought the traffic was an aberration. I would spend three times longer getting anywhere than I'd estimated, complain loudly the whole time, and arrive late and annoyed. My stock of in-car swear words grew alarmingly.

Now, I take the traffic as a given, allow an appropriate amount of time, bring supplies (food, blankets, and reading materials—well, a cup of coffee at least), and avoid certain times of the day at all cost.

Why am I telling you all this? Well, there's an important analogy here with what's happening with employee retention.

As we saw in Chapter 1, retention strategies used to be based on the status quo model. This assumed that there was a "normal," "acceptable" rate of employee retention and that low retention rates were bad and relatively unusual. This is just like my original view of the San Francisco traffic—"This is terrible, and the sooner it gets back to normal, the better."

Then time passes, with the same traffic problems, the same loss of good employees, until you slowly realize that retention, like the traffic on 101, is not going to get any better! It's an axiom of our age: "Constant change is here to stay."

So the first and most important thing you can do is to change the way you look at retention issues. Managing retention, like driving where I live, isn't about stopping the traffic; it's about going with the flow. You can no more stop the mobility of good people than I can hurry the traffic on Highway 101. Job mobility is a function of upskilling and economic growth: you cannot (and should not) stop it.

## Think Like a Diner Owner

Once you accept that employee turnover is here to stay, that job mobility is a given and no longer an aberration, the next thing to do is to make your workplace attractive to people on the move.

Think about a diner located along a busy highway, with all those potential customers driving past. If the owner of the diner is smart, what does she do? Simply wait for the customers to stop? Of course not. She makes the diner attractive: she puts up signs, she maintains the property, she puts out tables. She does whatever it takes to bring in the customers.

Look around at your hiring practices, your publicity materials, and your working environment. There are a lot of good people out there who notice the presence and image of your company. Do they see a workplace that's welcoming, that beckons to them? Or do they see an environment that's defensive, insular, preoccupied with not losing its employees?

Good employees are on the move, sure, but they're on the move to somewhere. Why not to your organization? What are

### Don't Focus on the Wrong Thing

Too many managers focus on how to stop people from leaving their company. That's wrong. As job mobility increases, your retention efforts are more likely to fail if you focus only on impeding exits.

Instead, focus on attracting the right people. Then, if the environment and the job are right for them, they'll stay for a "natural" length of time. Don't expect even the best fit to work forever. Just make the most of the skills and interests of each employee for as long as he or she stays with you.

you doing to attract the right people?

### Go Roadside

My Dad is a great fisherman. The secret of his success? "I go where the fish are." It's as simple as that.

You want good people. Good people are on the move. So, where should you be? Where the good people are—right on the roadside, right by that flow of traffic. That means not only accepting employee mobility, but actively working with it.

Identify your top employees and get to know and understand them. What skills and personality traits make them the best? What are their interests? From what you know about those employees, you may be able to determine where to find similar prospects. Then, that's where you recruit or at least establish your organization's presence and image.

### Use Your Computer to Go Roadside

If you haven't already done so, get on the Internet. It's probably the busiest "employee highway."

Familiarize yourself with recruiting Web sites like www.monster.com, free agent Web sites like www.guru.com, and HR sites like www.hr.com.

Sign up for online "ezines" (e-mail newsletters). The sites above offer them, as do industry-specific sites such as Electronic Recruiting Exchange at www.erexchange.com/forum/, which covers all things recruiting and the Internet. Test-drive five or six until you find a couple you like; then unsubscribe from those that don't meet your needs. Your aim is to become familiar with how potential employees use the Internet. In later chapters we'll examine other ways to use the Internet to improve retention.

### Think Velcro, Not Erector

Employer-employee relationships used to be like those Erector sets from Meccano, that great stuff we played with as kids— metal girders, gears, bolts and nuts, screwdrivers—solid, structural things that clanged when you touched them. The "status quo" relationship meant that employees were attached to the company and to each other, forming a sort of semi-permanent structure.

In the world of increased job mobility, employer-employee relationships are more like Velcro—easy on, easy off. In developing your retention mindset, it's vital that you learn to look at employer-employee relationships in this way: pliable, supple, and reusable.

## Don't Get Hung Up on Strategies

After developing a retention mindset and accepting that employee mobility is here to stay, the second perception change that's needed is in regard to the retention strategy you're going to design by working through this book.

The perception change is this: your retention strategy is the *vehicle*, not the *destination*.

A strategy will not of itself make any sustainable difference in retention in the long term. What will make a difference is not the strategy, but the changes that it makes in your organization.

When did you last hear someone say, "The reason I stayed with this company is because they have a great retention strategy"? In fact, when was the last time you heard anyone in a relationship of any kind (and employment is a relationship at heart) say that he or she stayed in the relationship because the other party had a great retention strategy? If your best friend told you, "I've held onto my significant other by using a retention strategy," what would you think of your friend? People stay with people because of who they are—not because of any "strategy."

It's no different in the employer-employee relationship—people stay with an organization because of what the organization is, not because of any strategy it may have.

## Make It Real

**Smart Managing** As you make notes while working through this book, don't think in terms of just building a "retention strategy." People don't respond to strategies; they respond to what's behind them. Think about how you can genuinely make your organization a place where people feel at home. As you adopt and adapt tips and techniques from this book to build that environment, you will end up with more than a retention strategy. You'll end up with a retention *culture*—a retention *way of life*.

Now, don't get me wrong. I'm not against strategies. In fact, this book is entirely directed to helping you construct an employee retention strategy. But if the strategy doesn't result in real, sustained changes in the organizational culture, then it will fail. A retention strategy that doesn't impact the organization is simply an attempt to manipulate employees— and it's doomed to failure.

Let's face it: employees don't care about "retention strategies." What they care about is staying somewhere they feel at home.

## People Stay Where They Feel at Home

I've already used this phrase in the previous section and will do so again, many times: people stay where they feel at home. This phrase is at the heart of effective retention.

Think about that "significant other." Think about your employees. Think about yourself, in your own job at present. Do any of these people—including you—stay where they are now because of a "retention strategy"? No.

People stay where they feel at home. As we'll show later, this applies to everyone you hire—from the most loyal, company-centered employee to the most ruthless, money-oriented mercenary you employ. We *all* stay where we feel at home.

### Retention Isn't Compulsion

The approach of many ineffectual retention strategies is "people will stay if we make them feel at home."

## "Home" Means Different Things to Different People

**Smart Managing**

We all stay where we feel at home—but the definition of "home" varies from person to person.

I'm not suggesting that you find out what "home" means to every one of your employees and then try to twist your organization into some sort of chameleon-like "all-things-to-all-people" paradise!

What's important is that you find out what sort of "home" your organization is. Knowing this will help you recruit and retain people who feel at home in your organization. All your retention activities will be impacted by this hugely important but very simple concept—that you aim to fit square pegs in square holes. We'll develop this idea further in Chapter 7.

Well, the problem is, you can't make people feel at home—they either feel at home or they don't.

Imagine that a friend invites you to spend the weekend. You arrive, but then find that the room where you're staying is freezing and you're left to take care of your own meals. You decide on Saturday evening that you've had enough and you're leaving. Your friend notices your annoyance (and packed bags) and, with a considerable effort, turns on the heat and starts making you dinner. Do you suddenly feel at home? Of course not—you remember the way you were treated earlier and it's unlikely that you'll be staying.

Similarly, either an organization has a welcoming environment or it doesn't. It's hard to fake. Successful retention isn't about doing things to make employees stay—it's about becoming a genuinely welcoming place,

## Words Make a Difference

**CAUTION!**

Be careful if you find yourself using imperative words such as "make," "cause," or "retain" when it comes to employee relations. Even "retention" itself is a poor word (though we use it here, to avoid confusion). With its overtones of "holding onto," "retention" implies that you're grabbing and clinging to employees to keep them from leaving. Effective retention is when your employees make a voluntary decision to stay, not when you hold them.

**Great Place to Work Institute**

If you have trouble making a start, try logging on to www.greatplacetowork.com. These are the folks who do the detailed analysis for the *Fortune* magazine "Top 100 Places to Work in America" list (and similar lists featured in other magazines). The whole site is worth visiting, but particularly www.greatplacetowork.com/ gptw/model.html. The model is based on credibility, respect, fairness, pride, and camaraderie. That should help you with the sorts of words used to describe places where employees love to work.

where employees choose to stay rather than leave.

Write down the words that best describe your organization. What makes it feel like "home"? What are the characteristics of your company that you're most proud of, the characteristics that first attracted you, that inspire, encourage, and move you?

You should be able to list five to 10 words that describe your company. Then, keep your list handy while you work through the rest of the book.

Are you having problems putting together a list of "home words"? If so, you've hit the first important issue in your battle against retention. If you cannot—with ease—state what it is about your organization that makes it feel like home, you'll have a problem getting people to stay.

You may want to consider calling together fellow managers for an hour or so to discuss this issue. Don't make it a big deal; just say you want their advice in developing a profile of the type of person who's most likely to stay with the company over time. Tease out your colleagues' views over a cup of coffee. Ask them to go through the exercise above. You will probably find that your colleagues will have a different take on the issue and they may be able to easily provide you with a list of "home words."

## The Five Phases of Retaining Top Employees: How Good Is Your Swing?

OK, we've tweaked our retention mindset, seen the importance of not depending too much on strategies, and established that people stay where they feel at home. Now it's time to get down to building a retention culture, a place where people want to stay.

The rest of this chapter outlines the steps we'll be taking and points to the appropriate chapters for details. From here on, we'll be talking less about employee retention in general and focusing more specifically on retaining top employees.

I'm not a great one for sports analogies—and I'm not that great at golf—but over the years I've noted something about successful golfers that underpins the successful approach I've used in working with top employees. Retaining top employees is very similar to developing a winning golf swing. There are five very separate phases:

1. **Picturing the Shot.** Great golfers always know where they're going to hit the ball; they don't just close their eyes and hope for the best. Similarly, for an effective retention strategy, you need to start by establishing your specific goals.
2. **Club Selection.** Next, it's essential to choose the right golf club to achieve the desired result. Effective retention uses the most appropriate tools to achieve realistic goals.
3. **Backswing.** After picturing the shot and selecting the club, it's time to hit the ball. The action begins with the backswing. This equates to an organization's recruitment activities—everything that happens before the hire.
4. **Point of Impact.** This is when and where the club head hits the ball. It's like the point of hire—the crucial first few days that an employee spends with the organization.
5. **Follow-Through.** After hitting the ball, the golfer continues the swing to provide accuracy and distance. The follow-through in retention is the ongoing managing, mentoring, and coaching of the employee.

Let's look at each of these five phases in turn.

## Picturing the Shot: Envisioning Your Retention Strategy

The fundamental prerequisite to a great golf shot is to visualize it exactly. Great golfers take time to consider exactly where they're going to hit the ball, taking into account how the contours of the course will affect the way the ball will bounce and roll.

It's the same for your retention program: the better you can specify the exact results you wish to achieve, the closer you'll come to achieving them and the more likely your interventions will make a positive, sustainable difference in retaining key employees.

## Acquiring Local Knowledge

In picturing golf shots, there's a great benefit in what's termed "local knowledge." Golfers who are playing on their home course know every bump and hollow, so they're able to picture their shots much more accurately than golfers who've never played that course before.

It's much the same with employee retention. It's one thing to just toss a retention initiative into the work environment and hope for a positive effect. It's quite another to fully understand the "bumps and hollows" of your organization, the "local knowledge" that ensures your retention-related activities have the right effects.

The best way to acquire local knowledge of a golf course is to play it, over and over again. Visiting golfers don't have that opportunity, so they do something called "walking the course." Before a tournament, professional golfers will walk every inch of the course, practicing shots from every angle, playing every bump and hollow, testing the course to see how it responds to different shots and in different conditions. The more successful the golfer, the more time he or she will have spent testing, testing, testing.

> **TRICKS OF THE TRADE**   **Walk the Course**
> To better understand your work environment, to get the "lay of the land," talk with your employees. What makes them want to stay around? What might cause them to feel less at home? What might eventually cause them to leave? The more perspectives you get, the better you can understand your environment.

For you, the equivalent to "walking the course" is

asking questions. You'll understand more and more about the likely effect of your retention-related activities by asking those directly involved—the employees. Every time you ask a relevant question of an employee and receive a valid answer, it's like pitching a golf ball onto a tricky hillock and seeing how it runs. Interviews are your equivalent of "walking the course." You must incorporate these into your retention-related activities. (We'll describe how to use interviews in your retention planning in Chapter 3.)

In Chapter 3 we'll examine in detail what it means to "picture the shot"—how to visualize and plan the exact retention strategy that's right for you.

## Club Selection: Deciding Which Retention Tools to Use

After visualizing the shot, a golfer selects the appropriate club to achieve the result visualized: a driver for the tee shot, a putter for the green, a sand wedge for getting out of bunkers, and so on. To retain top employees, you must choose the right tools to achieve your goals. The possibilities are numerous: compensation schemes, crèches, pension plans, cars, bonuses, fresh paint, coaching, 360-degree assessments, barbecues ... to name just a few.

How can you decide which tools are exactly right to achieve your specific retention goals? The answer is twofold:

1. Benchmark against the results other organizations have achieved with a specific tool, so you can estimate the result likely in your organization.
2. Pilot-test a specific tool, so you can observe the outcome directly in a controlled environment, before implementing it throughout the organization.

In Chapters 4 through 6 we'll take a detailed look at how to select the right tools for your retention goals, the specific interventions to produce the results you want.

## Backswing: Recruiting for Retention

After visualizing the shot and selecting the right club, it's time to take action. That begins with the backswing. Lesser golfers tend to overlook the importance of the backswing—and their game suffers as a result.

In retention, the backswing is every recruiting activity we undertake before hiring a prospect. Two aspects of the recruitment process impact effective retention—how the organization hires and the impression made during the recruitment process.

### Using the Right Hiring Model

The changes in the underlying "employment contract" that we saw in Chapter 1—particularly the move away from the traditional "status quo" model, the growth of outsourcing, and the rise of the free agent—have resulted in a number of alternative "hiring models."

In addition to the classic "core employee"—a full-time employee in a single job—we have alternative hiring models such as job sharing, flexible working, telecommuting, contracting, etc. An essential element of retention is choosing the best hiring models to match employee preferences with the tasks to be performed. Using the wrong hiring models will result in stressed, unproductive employees and high turnover.

In Chapter 7 we look in detail at the various hiring models and how and why to use each.

### Communicating Consistently

As we saw above, effective retention begins before the employee joins the organization. It starts with every image, every message, every impression the organization conveys in the marketplace.

Every potential employee is first a member of the general public, impacted by the organization's overall image just like everyone else, forming impressions and making conscious and subconscious decisions based on everything he or she sees and hears about you before and after the hire—not just on your carefully controlled post-hire "employee communications."

> ## Review Your Image
>
> **Smart Managing**
>
> Gather an assortment of messages that the public could get about your organization—brochures, product literature, press releases, advertisements, articles, and so on. If you have a Web site, print out sample pages. Use a search engine to look up references and links to your organization.
>
> Next, sit down somewhere quiet where you won't be interrupted and immerse yourself in those messages. Try to put yourself in the shoes of the general public. What overall impressions are you getting about the organization?
>
> Now, look at the materials again, this time as a potential employee. What messages are you getting now? If you were starting work next week, what assumptions, suppositions, and expectations would you bring from all those messages?
>
> If it's hard to be objective about the materials you've gathered, ask a friend who doesn't work for your organization to do the same exercise with those materials and give you feedback.

Effective retention begins with these very first impressions. Inconsistency between the messages you give to the world and the messages employees receive within your organization is one of the root causes of employee turnover—and it's too late to do anything about it after you've hired .

In Chapter 8 we'll examine the key messages your organization sends to potential employees, how they interpret those messages, what to do to ensure that those message have a positive effect on retention, and how to harmonize what you're saying to employees pre-hire and post-hire.

## Point of Impact: Making the Difference with Orientation

Something interesting occurs at the point of impact between a golf club and the ball. If the face of the club is aligned improperly, even by just a millimeter, the ball can easily end up 10, 50, or 100 yards from our target.

So it is with retention. Once you've set your goals, selected the right tools, and communicated effectively before hiring, the

> **Orientation Is Not Induction**
>
> It's important to distinguish between *orientation* and *induction*. Induction (in-processing, form-filling, benefits and compensation details, health and safety instruction) is all about giving people tools. Orientation is showing employees what you want them to achieve with the tools.
>
> There's little about the induction process that's inherently related to retention. Induction tends to be technical, mechanical, or legislatively driven (and often boring!). Orientation, on the other hand, is where the organization imparts direction to the new employee. Concentrating on induction at the expense of orientation is detrimental to effective retention.

point of impact arrives—the person joins the organization. It's at this crucial point—during the new employee's first few days—that the organization sets the direction in which the employee will travel. If you're out of alignment with your key employees at this point, it should be no surprise if weeks, months, or years later you find that you've missed your retention target. The key to ensuring that employees start off in the right direction toward your retention goal is effective orientation.

Effective orientation is usually the very first high-impact intervention managers can make to influence the retention of key employees. Most orientation programs are minimal or poorly executed; the effect on retention is negligible or even negative. Other programs are "almost there"—a few minor "tweaks" can make an enormous difference weeks and months down the line.

In Chapter 9 we will examine the vital components your orientation program must have in order to maximize your retention of key employees.

## Follow-Through: Maintaining Retention Through the Employment Life Cycle

Any decent golfer knows that following through on the swing is vital to get the ball to end up on target. A strong follow-through improves the distance and accuracy of the shot.

---

### Use Performance Management Tools

Do you know the organizational goals that you want every employee to achieve? Do you and your employees know if they're hitting those goals?

If not, employees may feel over time like they haven't accomplished enough. This feeling of malaise or even of failure may cause employees to leave in hopes of feeling more fulfilled somewhere else.

A good performance management process can help improve retention in two ways:

1. Use job descriptions or annual reviews to state the goals that each employee is expected to achieve year by year.
2. Use performance appraisal mechanisms to measure the progress of employees toward those goals.

(We'll explore the role of performance management in employee retention in more detail in Chapter 10.)

---

It's just the same with employee retention: after your recruiting and pre-hire messaging begins the employer-employee relationship and your orientation provides initial direction, your follow-through will improve distance (the length of that employer-employee relationship) and accuracy (the degree to which the employee will meet overall organizational goals). Both distance and accuracy are vital. There's little point in working hard to retain an employee for a long time if he or she is contributing little to your organizational objectives!

There are two main elements in a strong follow-through. One is the employee's manager or supervisor, by supervising, directing, and instructing the employee. In this way, the manager ensures accuracy—achieving organizational goals. The other is the employee's mentor and/or coach, by supporting, encouraging, and advising. The mentor or coach ensures distance—helping the employee stay, grow, and develop over time.

In Chapters 10 and 11 we will look at employee retention follow-through—the role of the manager, mentor, and coach—and we'll see how managers, mentors, and coaches work together to produce enduring, productive employee-employer relationships—relationships with distance and accuracy.

## Manager's Checklist for Chapter 2

❏ Employee mobility is here to stay. We cannot resist it. We must learn to manage it.

❏ Employees don't get excited about "retention strategies." People stay where they feel at home.

❏ The first step in effective retention is to set clear goals.

❏ The retention "tools" you use must be appropriate to achieve those goals.

❏ Retention starts with recruitment: what you say and do before you hire is as important as what you say and do after you hire.

❏ Effective orientation is vital to starting employees off in the right direction.

❏ Management, mentoring, and coaching combine to keep the employee on the right path over time.

# Envisioning Your Retention Strategy

*Obstacles are those frightful things you see when you take your eyes off your goal.*
—Henry Ford

The clearer your goals, the more successful your employee retention strategy will be. Conversely, the cloudier your goals, the more obstacles you're likely to encounter trying to achieve them. In this chapter, we'll learn how to set achievable retention goals through four steps:

1. Identify the employees you want to retain.
2. Clarify why you want to retain them.
3. Discover what you need to do to retain them.
4. Use all of the above to set clear, measurable goals for your retention strategy.

## Which Employees Do You Want to Retain?

The first step in designing an effective retention strategy for top performers is to decide which employees to target as "at risk"—

**Envision This ...**

Take the example of Jones Painterson & Co, a medium-sized accounting firm with 2000 employees.

Jane, the partner in charge of the Tax Department, has cleared her desk to address the issue of retaining key employees. After working through the steps in this chapter, she arrives at a few conclusions:

- The main retention issue is with the senior managers in the Tax Department.
- The main reason she wants to retain them is that the clients are becoming increasingly upset at having to deal with new senior staff every year.
- The main reason for this retention issue is the relatively young age of the partners in the Tax Department, meaning that senior managers are unlikely to earn promotion to partner in the foreseeable future, so they're more susceptible to being enticed elsewhere with promises of partnership.

Jane decides that an achievable goal is to reduce the turnover of senior tax managers from 34% to 10% within two years.

in need of particular attention. Which employees do you want to keep?

This question may seem stupid or at least politically incorrect. Surely the answer is "All of them."

After all, aren't we expected to be caring, inclusive employers, treating everyone from the receptionist to the CEO exactly the same? Isn't retention vital for *every* employee? At the very least, don't we want to retain *all* our *top* performers?

Well, that may seem like a great idea, but there are at least four reasons why it isn't realistic:

- **It just isn't so.** Most organizations don't want to retain all employees. There are almost always at least a few "standouts" who could leave without causing many tears. There may even be some top performers who are such mavericks that their stellar performance is too high a price to pay for the disruption they cause.
- **"If it ain't broke, don't fix it."** If the employees in your marketing division or in your Carolina office or working on Project Blue are a perfectly happy, well-integrated

group, you don't want to disturb anything with an unnecessary "retention strategy." If you misjudge the climate within your organization or a particular unit and put strategies in place where retention is not a problem, you'll confuse your employees and they'll believe that management is out of touch and insincere.

- **Resources go only so far.** For most managers, targeting resources on a narrowly defined, key group that will benefit most from them is much wiser stewardship than spraying resources across all their employees and hoping some of it sticks. Your want to focus resources where you can get "the most bang for your buck."
- **It's easier.** As we've seen, there are a lot of variables at play in retention. Truly understanding what's going on with any one group of employees and coming up with the best response can be complicated and time-consuming. Anything you can do to simplify the situation, like dealing with one key group at a time, is going to improve the quality of your decision-making.

## Identifying Key Retention Groups

So, which employees do you target first when you set retention goals? Sometimes the answer to this question is obvious; sometimes it's less so.

### Managing Mavericks

Smart Managing

It's not uncommon for an organization to find that some of its top performers are not top team players or that they're so lacking in some other business (or social) skills that their status as top performers is the only thing keeping them in the organization.

It's very unwise to develop a retention strategy to specifically target such individuals, for two reasons:
- By implication, it encourages wrong behavior.
- It seriously undermines the motivation of their fellow employees, who wonder why the organization is trying so hard to retain people so difficult to work with.

If you're in this position, consider using a mentoring or coaching program first, to deal with the employees' underlying skills deficit, before involving the employees in a retention program.

You may have picked up this book because of a concern about a group of employees you've already identified. In that case, you've got a great starting point—although you should complete this section anyway, to make sure you haven't missed anything.

But maybe you're just concerned in general that "we should be doing something about keeping our best folks." If so, here's a four-step guide to identifying where you should focus your employee retention activities.

**The squeaky wheel.** The simplest way (and the most common) to see where to begin focusing your retention activities is to listen to what your fellow managers and the senior executives are saying. If every time you bump into your CEO or a divisional head, you hear, "You have to do something to keep more of your corporate account sales managers," well, there's a pretty good indication right there. Sometimes oiling that squeaky wheel is the most obvious starting point!

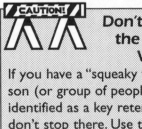

**Don't Stop with the Squeaky Wheel**

If you have a "squeaky wheel"—a person (or group of people) already identified as a key retention group—don't stop there. Use the remaining three points in this section to check for other key retention groups to include in your employee retention strategy. The squeaky wheel may get the grease, but it may not be the only wheel that needs it.

**The obvious gap.** Like the squeaky wheel, this key retention group is usually not difficult to spot. This is the group of employees in which there are *always* outstanding unfilled positions. This key retention group stares out at you from the organization chart with "TBA" ("to be appointed") as the most common entry. It's hard to find people to fill these key positions (we'll discuss reasons later in the chapter) and, when you do, it's hard to keep them.

Note: These first two categories often overlap, but not always. It's important to watch for the situation where they *don't* overlap. Sometimes the squeaky wheels squeak about the obvious gap, sometimes not. If the obvious gap stays unfilled for some time, the squeaky wheels can go quiet, a sure sign of some degree of acceptance of the situation. Don't let a quiet obvious gap fool you. Quiet gaps are even more important than noisy ones, because they indicate that managers have stopped trying to fix them.

### Nurses

A good example of an obvious gap is the current shortage of qualified nurses. In some hospitals this obvious gap has become dangerously quiet, as hospital administrators have stopped complaining about it. It's still a problem (and even growing in recent years), but because it's been a gap for so long there doesn't seem much point in complaining any more!

In most hospitals, nurses are a key retention group, having moved from the squeaky wheel category to the obvious gap in the last few years.

**Follow the money.** If there's no squeaky wheel or obvious gap in your part of the organization, then the easiest way to identify your key retention group is to "follow the money." Look carefully at employee groups with any of the following characteristics:

- High recruitment cost per head
- High training cost per head
- High one-time (unplanned) discretionary or other performance bonuses

These generally indicate an employee group where positions *are* filling (unlike the obvious gap), but the turnover rate is high.

**Keep a dream diary.** The final key retention group is the hardest to spot. The three other groups are *already* causing retention difficulties, so they're on your "radar screen." Equally important to address, but harder to spot, are those employee categories that *could* cause major problems in the future.

To identify this very important key retention group, think through your worst nightmares. Which group of employees would cause you to stay up at night if suddenly there was an exodus?

**Future Risks**

Our biotech company may have a perfectly acceptable relationship with its group of key R&D scientists, but it would be exceptionally vulnerable if those employees decided to leave the organization, individually or as a group.

Since they remain dedicated and loyal while working on Project XYZ, they may never appear on the "squeaky wheel," "obvious gap," or "follow the money" scorecards. But deep in their departmental VP's subconscious, there may well lurk a fear about what would happen if they all decided to leave.

## Why Do You Want to Retain the Targeted Employees?

Now, it may seem that I'm specializing in stupid questions in the chapter, but the next question to ask, after you've identified your key retention groups, is "*Why* do you want to retain them?"

There are almost always two answers to this question:

- Resources: it's too expensive, in cash and time, to hire a top performer every few months.
- Recruitment: top employees are hard to get.

While these reasons are usually valid, it's important to check for any additional *operational* reasons for focusing on a key retention group. Uncovering additional reasons at this point will enable you to plan your retention strategy for maximum impact. Consider the following two examples.

### Example: The Knowledge Management Need

In the case of the biotech company with R&D scientists, the *underlying* issue faced by the organization, beyond the cost and effort of replacing key employees, is *knowledge management*. The company is extremely vulnerable to the loss of institutional knowledge if the members of the project team choose to leave, individually or as a group. It's important that the retention strategy for the key chemists also address the issue of trapping and managing the vital information that the chemists are generating

> **Institutional knowledge**  The knowledge and information
> gathered by an organization that forms an integral part of its
> asset base and that it uses to create value and make a profit
> or otherwise fulfill its mission.
>   Institutional knowledge can be either trapped within the organiza-
> tion (and therefore independent of any individual) or held by individu-
> als (and therefore dependent on those individuals). As they've moved
> away from the status quo relationship with their employees, many
> organizations have discovered that their assets are now traveling up
> and down in elevators and leaving the building every night.

(using a computer database or a buddy system, for example).

### Example: The Unhappy Clients

Let's return to Jones Painterman & Co., the accounting firm
with high turnover of senior tax managers. You'll recall that the
underlying problem is not just the cost and effort of replacing
key employees, but the dissatisfaction expressed by clients who
must work with different managers. Reducing turnover will be a
great achievement for Jane, the partner in charge, but it won't
solve her problem of unhappy clients. Even when she gets senior tax managers to stay with the firm, she'll still have to deal
with unhappy clients if ever those tax managers are assigned to
other clients, get sick, or move to other duties within the firm.

To reduce the possibility of dissatisfaction, Jane might
include in her goals to design a system to give clients two senior points of contact—a tax manager and an assignment manager, for example—to ensure continuity should the tax manager
leave the assignment for any reason.

### Determining the Reasons for Retaining Top Employees

Finding out the underlying reasons can take some investigation.
It's not always obvious if there's a key operational issue involved,
apart from the resource and recruitment costs. It's also seduc-
tively easy to focus on the resource and recruitment implications—cost of hiring, retraining, lost production or sales, etc.—
because these costs are usually readily obtained. However, for
your retention strategy to have maximum effect, it must isolate

and deal with the operational issues as well as the employee issues.

To establish the main operational issues caused by the loss (or potential loss) of any key employee, take the perspective of the key employee's clients. We don't mean (necessarily) the organization's clients or customers, though they might be included. The clients could be the employee's manager or supervisor, other staff, suppliers, agencies, customers—whoever the employee most impacts.

Once you've identified the key employee's client, put yourself in the client's place. Try to get inside his or her mindset and think about the main impact of losing that key employee. Talk with the client, if you can do so without raising eyebrows, and ask the question, "How are you most impacted by turnover in this key position?"

We've already seen some examples—the tax managers whose departure leaves unhappy clients and the R&D scientists who cause a "knowledge vacuum" when they leave. What about the CEO's assistant? The in-house attorney? What is the main operational impact on their clients if they should leave?

**Key Term**  **Employee clients** The individuals or organizations for which the employee provides the most added value.

For instance, an in-house attorney for a toy manufacturer might have as his main client the marketing department, for which he must obtain copyright and patenting clearance before a product can be sold. The main client for the tax manager in Jones Painterman & Co. is probably the end customer, for whom she must perform timely and accurate assignments. The main client for an assistant to the CEO is almost certainly the CEO.

If you have trouble ascertaining the employee clients for a specific key retention group, an excellent way to get an overview is with an "added value chart"—a sort of loose organizational chart with lines indicating the flow of added value among employees. You can use the techniques in Tony Buzan's excellent book, *The Mind Map Book: How to Use Radiant Thinking to Maximize Your Brain's Untapped Potential* (Plume/Penguin, 1996), to help you produce such a chart.

Whatever it is, you will want to identify that impact and incorporate it into your retention strategy for maximum effect.

### Map the Targeted Employee Groups and Their Operational Impact

At this stage, it's probably a good idea to produce a table summarizing what you've identified so far. The format isn't crucial; what's important is that you record your findings in a way that makes sense to you. Figure 3-1 shows an example of what you might produce.

| Target Employee or Group | How Identified | Why We Want to Retain Them |
|---|---|---|
| R&D Scientists Grade VII | Discussion with VP R&D *(dream diary)* | Loss of institutional knowledge |
| Senior Tax Managers | Large expenditures in last year on recruiting and training *(follow the money)* | Dissatisfied clients |
| Greg Doitall, Assistant to the CEO | Constant reminders from CEO *(squeaky wheel)* | ? |
| In-House Attorney | Haven't had one for six months *(obvious gap)* | ? |

Figure 3-1. Table for gathering data

Take a shot at what might be put in the "Why We Want to Retain Them" column for the two final entries, then use the blank rows to jot down your initial thoughts on what employee groups are key, how you know they're key, and what their main operational impact might be.

## What Do You Need to Do to Retain the Targeted Employees?

We've now arrived at the third step in envisioning your employee retention strategy. You've identified who you want to retain and why you want to retain them. Now it's time to find out why there's a retention problem.

The best way to answer the question "Why do we have a retention problem?" is to get out of the office and ask people, particularly the people most impacted by it. Charts, graphs, and statistics help tell us *what* has happened historically regarding turnover, but they aren't "rich data" when it comes to figuring out *why* you have a retention problem.

You can't design an effective retention strategy, particularly one targeting top performers, from behind a desk. An essential part of the process is meeting people and conducting meaningful interviews that will help us come to accurate conclusions. So, who should we meet and what should we ask?

### The Exit Interview: Most Used, Least Effective

Most managers are familiar with the concept of the *exit interview*—debriefing departing or recently departed employees to learn their reasons for leaving. This seems like a natural and useful thing to do. After all, grappling with retention issues starts with understanding why people are leaving, so we should do exit interviews, right?

Well, not necessarily. It depends on the type and quality of the information you want to receive. While exit interviews provide useful anecdotal information, if you want to establish hard, measurable facts, you need to handle the exit interview with care. Here's why:

- The benefit of finding out why people leave is limited unless you understand why they joined. It's important to compare what people say when they're leaving and what they said when they joined, to see what's changed in between.
- Most people leaving a job don't want to rock the boat or burn bridges. Sometime they might need a reference or even return for a job. So responses in exit interviews can be somewhat restrained.
- People who are leaving a job rationalize their decision. To avoid feeling remorse about leaving, they think of all the positive reasons for taking the new job. This makes the

responses to the classic exit interview question "Why are you leaving?" somewhat suspect.

If you choose to conduct an exit interview, don't ask that old question, "Why are you leaving?" Even if your departing employees tell the truth (and most come prepared with a standard, bland response), you still won't get the answers you want.

Instead, ask, "Why didn't you stay?"

This question may seem semantically similar, but it's crucially different. For one thing, it deflects the prepared, standard response. But, more important, it changes the focus of the employee's answer.

What can you do to get more useful information from exit interviews? Here are a few tips.

### Have the Interviews Facilitated Externally

No matter how good you think you are at interviewing, for all the reasons detailed above you will not get reliable information from exit interviews—even if HR or staff from other functional departments do the interviews. Your departing employee will still assume that the information will come back to you, as his or her former manager.

To improve the quality of information garnered from exit interviews, get someone external to the organization to conduct

**Why Are You Leaving?" vs. "Why Didn't You Stay?"**

Ask Joe Leaver, "Why are you leaving?" He thinks long, decides to tell the truth, drops his prepared response, gulps, and says, "My manager was a bully."

Is that what you really need to know? You may think so. However, let's say you ask, "Well, accepting that, why didn't you stay?" Joe thinks harder, then says, "I guess it's because when I complained about my manager's bullying, nobody did anything about it. I'm a big guy. I could take the petty bullying. What I couldn't take was the company's apathy about it."

Do you see the difference? "Why are you leaving?" will uncover the ailment. "Why didn't you stay?" uncovers the cure you need to implement.

### Improve Results with Confidentiality

You want departing employees to tell "the truth, the whole truth, and nothing but the truth." That may be difficult for many of them, for various reasons. Make it easier by using an independent outsider and ensuring that whatever employees say during the exit interview will be kept confidential. After all, you probably do not need to know the specifics of any individual's experience. You're looking for evidence of trends—generic issues that recur regularly.

them and then summarize the responses for you. Explain to employees that the independent interviewer will providing general information only, that no one in your organization will see any specifics. If possible, you might also provide a printed assurance of confidentiality, signed by a senior management representative.

## Conduct Entry Interviews as Well as Exit Interviews

As mentioned above, to really make sense of exit interview information, it's essential to have a benchmark for comparing the responses. You can construct one by conducting an *entry interview* when any employee joins your group.

The structure for an entry interview is much the same as for an exit interview: Have an external party consistently interview your new hires to find out why they joined your company. You can build this into your orientation program. (See Chapter 8.)

Again, assure the new hires that the third party will keep all information confidential and give you composite summaries of information provided during the interviews. Use that information to track correlations between why people are joining and why they are leaving.

Here's an example. Your entry interviews reveal that 65% of your hires give as one of the reasons for joining your organization its reputation as "a fun place to work." In exit interviews, 62% say that one of their reasons for leaving is "a negative atmosphere in their workplace." You can conclude that the messages being conveyed during the recruitment process don't match the reality the employees find on the job.

### The Most Important Interview: Why Are You Staying?

Amazingly, the single best method of acquiring quality information about the retention of key performers isn't used at all by most organizations. As we've already seen, many organizations undertake extensive exit interviews. Some organizations also conduct entry interviews, giving a baseline for interpreting the exit interview data. This provides good quality information about why employees leave.

> ### Online Surveys
> There are a number of excellent Web-based online survey tools—such as www.zoomerang.com and www.supersurvey.com—that enable you to construct your interviews online (and anonymously, if you so desire). Many of the online survey companies provide templates that you can use as a starting point for building your own survey. Go to your search engine of choice and key in "online survey software" to find out about the offerings available currently.

However, very few organizations ever take time to conduct the interview that will provide the most timely information about why their top performers are leaving or will leave—the "Why are you staying?" interview.

Exit interviews are post-mortems: they're conducted after the loss. Even if the information they produce is of high quality, acting on that information is a bit like locking the barn door after a horse has bolted. As a result, many of the retention strategies built on exit interview data are remedial—and they feel that way to the employees. Often, by the time a retention strategy based on exit interviews is put in place, the prevailing attitude among the remaining employees is "Sorry—too little, too late." Morale may already be so bad that a retention strategy meets with apathy at best and resentment at the extreme.

"Why are you staying?" interviews, on the other hand, are proactive rather than reactive. They enable you to anticipate those issues that could lead to a problem among your key retention groups.

For example, let's return to our fictitious biotech company. Imagine a series of "Why are you staying?" interviews with the R&D scientists. George, the Senior Scientist, receives a consolidated summary of the results and sees that the number-one answer to the question "Why are you still working for us?" is "Because in our field Project XYZ is one of the top five research projects in the world."

George has just received an exceptionally valuable, predictive glimpse into where he must focus his retention activities—developing exciting, career-enhancing projects to keep his scientists after Project XYZ is completed. How much better is it to know that information now, rather than later, from the exit interview after George loses one or more of his scientists?

The "Why are you staying?" interview must be conducted outside of the performance review process and ideally not by you as the employee's manager or supervisor. As noted for the other interviews, the value of the responses you receive will be much greater if the "stay" interviews are done by an outside interviewer and confidentiality is guaranteed.

### These Aren't Performance Reviews

Don't confuse "Why are you staying?" interviews with your regular performance reviews.

Your employees won't truthfully tell you why they're staying if they think the question has a punishment/reward implication. They'll tell you what they think you want to hear.

## Starting Right: The "Why Didn't You Join Us?" Interview

There's one specific type of retention problem that calls for yet another type of interview. That's the situation where our retention of top employees never even starts: a prospect chooses not to join the organization.

A chronic inability to hire high-caliber employees is really a very pronounced retention problem—so pronounced that even potential employees can spot it. There can be many reasons:

poor reputation in the marketplace, unattractive location, uncompetitive salaries. It's critical for you to uncover the reasons and deal with them expeditiously.

The simplest way to do this is to conduct a "Why didn't you join us?" interview. Find out why candidates declined your job offer.

As before, to get the best information, "Why didn't you join us?" interviews should be conducted by someone not directly connected to your organization and with an assurance of confidentiality. It's possible, of course, for you or someone else in the organization to conduct the interview, such as through a brief telephone survey by the HR staff, but the quality of the information received will be considerably lower.

### What to Ask in the Interviews

Designing a good interview structure that will yield high-quality information for retention planning is a circular process:

- You want to ask employees, potential employees, or former employees relevant questions about what really matters to them, *but*
- You don't know what really matters to them until we've completed the interview.

**Don't Let the Recruiters Do It**

Whoever conducts the "Why didn't you join us?" interviews, it should definitely *not* be the company recruiters. It's almost impossible for a recruiter, whether internal or external, to be detached enough to conduct such an interview objectively. Recruiters spend all their time "selling" the organization to potential employees; it's almost impossible to switch off the sales pitch and ask objectively about why a prospect has chosen not to join the organization.

Also, sometimes the very reason prospects do not accept your job offers may be the way in which the recruiter is doing his or her job. In that case, it can be very hard for the former prospects to give honest feedback—and hard for the recruiter to convey that information to others in the organization.

So it's important not to get hung up on the first draft of an interview questionnaire—and it's *vital* not to allow the first draft to become the final version. The first draft is merely a start in developing the final version—which should be revised later, as necessary, according to the results generated.

---

### Sample Exit Interview

Rate each item 1-5 (1 = Excellent, 2 = Good, 3 = Average, 4 = Poor, 5 = Very Bad):

Overall, ABC & Co. is a ___ place to work.

Company policies and procedures are ___.

My compensation and benefits package is ___.

My fringe benefits are ___.

ABC's commitment to employees is ___.

My manager's commitment to my personal development was ___.

The training I received here was ___.

The promotion opportunities available to me were ___.

My understanding of my job specification was ___.

The performance appraisal process here is ___.

Communication by senior management of organizational goals and objectives was ___.

The extent to which I was informed about changes in my job responsibilities was ___.

The recognition I received for doing a good job was ___.

My manager's willingness to listen to my problems and help me when I had difficulties or questions was ___.

My manager's willingness to accept suggestions I made was ___.

The opportunities I had to develop my potential were ___.

The level of teamwork among my colleagues was ___.

The specific projects I worked on were ___.

---

The sidebar shows a sample format for the survey element of an exit interview, with examples of typical questions.

For most employee surveys, appropriate questions will almost always revolve around the 4 P's—the people, the place, the project(s), and the pennies. Use the sample in the sidebar and those you find on the Internet (see sidebar, "Designing Interview Templates") to design your surveys.

---

### Designing Interview Templates

If you sit down with a blank sheet of paper to design an entry, exit, or other interview, it can be a daunting experience. However, with the profusion of information on the Internet, you can find literally hundreds of examples to use as a starting point for designing your own.

Go to any of the Web sites mentioned earlier in this chapter that offer Web-based surveys and you'll find an "employee survey" template. Or fire up your favorite search engine and key in "exit interview." (You'll even find sites that offer advice to employees on how to conduct themselves in exit interviews!)

With the Internet, the difficulty of starting with that blank sheet of paper is replaced by the difficulty of choosing among the hundreds of examples available.

---

## Turning Data into Achievable Retention Goals

Having worked through this chapter, you now know:

- Who you want to retain
- Why you want to retain them
- What you need to do to retain them

The final step at this stage is to turn that information into a set of achievable employee retention goals.

You should set goals that are *quantifiable* and *precise*. You've got to quantify what you want in order to be able to measure your progress. The more precise your goals are, the better you can measure the success of your efforts. If your goal is "reduce turnover among senior tax managers," for example, or "retain the existing R&D team," you're going to have trouble measuring your progress—or even deciding on your tactics.

> **Key Term**
>
> **Employee retention goals** The broad statement of what you would like to achieve for each key retention group. Your goals should be as *quantifiable* and *precise* as possible.

You need to refine those general goals: "reduce turnover among senior tax managers from 34% to 10% in a two-year period" or "retain the existing R&D team on Project XYZ intact until the product certification stage."

Be sure to distinguish between your *goals* and the *tactics* you

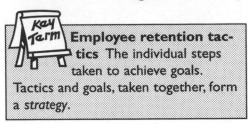

**Key Term** **Employee retention tactics** The individual steps taken to achieve goals. Tactics and goals, taken together, form a *strategy*.

will use to achieve those goals. (We'll discuss tactics—such things as compensation and benefits packages, bonuses, perks, status enhancements, bigger offices, better communication, more recognition, mentoring, and coaching—in Chapters 4, 5, and 6.)

The tactics you'll use will depend on the goals you establish in this chapter.

At this stage it's important to remain focused on the overall goals of your strategy; thinking about tactics before you've set your goals is rather like putting the cart before the horse. (However, there's no harm in noting any tactics that occur to you while you're establishing your goals or conducting your interviews. You never want to lose any ideas!)

The simplest way to summarize your retention goals is to extend the table we designed earlier, in Figure 3-1.

Figure 3-2 shows how the summary interview data is placed alongside the information collated earlier, with the overall goals in the right-hand column, together with some brief notes about specific tactical steps to explore later.

This table is obviously stylized and is a neat, hypothetical case study, with no loose ends. Your specific situation may well be rather more complex and you may go through many more drafts before deciding on a final set of goals. But nonetheless, the process is the same and the final outcome should be the same—quantifiable and precise goals.

## Manager's Checklist for Chapter 3

❏ Establish and prioritize the *key groups* that present a current or future retention risk.

| Target Employee or Group | How Identified | Main Operational Impact | Summary Interview Data | Suggested Retention Goals |
|---|---|---|---|---|
| R&D Scientists Grade VII | Discussion with VP R&D *(dream diary)* | Loss of institutional knowledge | The project is all. Enjoy working together as a team. *("Why are you staying?" and Entry)* | Keep team together until end of this project, about 16 months. *Tactical Note:* Establish next project well in advance. |
| Senior Tax Managers | Large expenditures last year on recruiting and training *(follow the money)* | Dissatisfied clients. | Our senior partners are young—limited promotion opportunity *(all interviews used)* | Fully staffed department (12 people) with employee turnover of less than 25%, within two years. *Tactical Note:* Can we create a new form of limited partner? |
| Greg Doitall, Assistant to the CEO | Constant reminders from CEO *(squeaky wheel)* | If Greg leaves, the CEO's productivity will drop sharply. | Enjoys the job, but lacks feedback and praise. ( *"Why are you staying?" and Exit – previous incumbent)* | Keep Greg until at least fall next year (end of Project XYZ). *Tactical Note:* CEO needs some coaching. |
| In-House Attorney | Haven't had one for six months. *(obvious gap)* | Bottleneck at product certification stage. | We have a reputation for doing a poor job on legal front. Unrewarding work. *(Exit and "Why didn't you take the job?")* | Redesign position to enable recruitment completion within six months. *Tactical Note:* Extend responsibilities to include corporate counsel. |

Figure 3-2. Table for setting retention goals

❏ For each key retention group, clarify reasons for wanting to retain them.

❏ With each group, use interviews (entry, exit, "Why didn't you take the job?" and "Why are you staying?") to ascertain what you need to do to retain the employees in that group.

❏ Make the interviews *independent* and *confidential* for best results.

❏ Use the information you've collected to establish clear, quantifiable retention goals for each group of employees.

❏ Note any retention *tactics* that emerge during the data collection process, but don't feel under pressure to map out the "whole campaign" at this stage.

# Know Your Demographics

*Born after the war, a baby of the boom,*
*The last generation allowed to slowly bloom.*
*I had a stay-at-home Mom, there every day,*
*Homemade cookies, when I came in from play.*
                    —Pamela Gayle Smith
                    "Lifespan of the Boomer Generation"

*Won't get fooled again.*
                    —Pete Townshend (The Who)

The vast majority of jobs in the workplace are currently held by members of one of two generations—the Baby Boomers and their successors, frequently referred to as Generation X. (Generation Y—people born after 1982—are only just entering the workforce, so we'll consider Gen-Yers only briefly at the end of this chapter.)

As with all generations, Boomers and Gen-Xers have distinctive features, preferences, and beliefs, many of which have affected their view of the workplace and impact materially on their retention. Attempting to retain a Gen-Xer using techniques that work for a Boomer is rather like playing your grandfather's favorite record to your 14-year-old child: an affinity in tastes is not impossible, but it's highly unlikely. A retention strategy that's attractive to

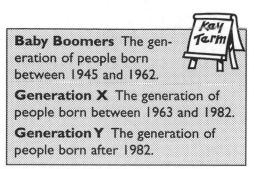

**Baby Boomers** The generation of people born between 1945 and 1962.

**Generation X** The generation of people born between 1963 and 1982.

**Generation Y** The generation of people born after 1982.

a Boomer can often seem like a version of purgatory to a Gen-Xer ... and vice versa.

In this chapter we'll examine the differences (and the similarities) between the techniques that work for Boomers and those that work for Gen-Xers.

## Boomers, Gen X, Gen Y: The More Things Change, the More They Stay the Same

The literature on generational differences is enormous and growing every day. Opinions and theories about what defines and distinguishes the generations are abundant.

### The Boomers Join ...

Beyond dispute is the fact that the Boomers grew up in the shadow of war: their parents lived through WWII, their grandpar-

---

**Sweeping Generalizations Ahead!**

In this chapter, broad, sweeping generalizations and not a little caricaturing are employed in order to make some points clearly and concisely.

Of course, not everyone born in any specific span of years demonstrates all of the characteristics I've attributed to the generations and there are few people who exactly fit the Boomer or Gen X profile. Additionally, there's a natural tendency (especially among the Gen-Xers) to resist attempts at categorization.

Nonetheless, demographic categorization is useful, if not vital, to efforts to improve retention of top employees. If you find in this chapter only one retention technique to amplify or downplay with your Boomers or Gen-Xers, then making the demographic distinction will have been worthwhile.

**Exploring the Generations**
If you're interested in discovering more about Boomers and Gen-Xers, here are two great places to start:
**www.boomercafe.com**—Described as "the Internet's most popular online magazine for baby boomers with active lifestyles," this e-zine has 400,000 readers.
**www.rainmakerthinking.com/63.htm**—Issues of *Generation X— The Workforce of the Future*, and a newsletter on Generation X, *Winning the Talent Wars*, are among the foremost resources for anyone seeking to understand this generation, from RainmakerThinking, Inc., founded by Bruce Tulgan, author of several books on Gen X and Gen Y.

ents lived through WW I, and as a generation they were directly involved in both the Korean and Vietnam wars.

For Boomers, respect for institutions and loyalty to their country and belief systems combined with relatively stable home lives (the incidence of divorce and two-working-parent families was still fairly low) to produce a generation often described as "joiners." Involved in social activities and group events, Boomers brought a heyday for local and community organizations such as the Scouts.

### The Gen-Xers Leave ...

For the generation born after 1962, a number of changes in socioeconomic conditions brought about a wholesale change in attitudes. Notable among these changes were the following:

- **The decline of the nuclear family**. With more working mothers and an increase in divorce, Gen-Xers had to be more self-sufficient earlier and in different ways than their parents or grandparents had experienced.
- **The rapid rise in the rate of change**. Exemplified in Alvin Toffler's classic 1970 book, *Future Shock*, Gen-Xers had to learn to deal with simultaneous, explosive changes in technology, legislation, the environment, the economy, and society as a whole.
- **Decline of monolithic institutions**. The breakup of the Soviet Union and the collapse of the Eastern Bloc symbol-

ized for many Gen-Xers their decline of respect for major institutions. This attitude developed during the 1970s and early '80s, when large companies laid off hundreds of thousands of employees in "rightsizing" realignments. The fact that many of those laid off were parents of Gen-Xers led members of that generation to become cynical about the loyalty previously exhibited by their parents, which seemed to them to have been misplaced.

### But in the End, People Are People

The life events detailed above produced a different set of attitudes and beliefs in each generation.

In order to examine those differences in detail, it's important to first establish a consistent framework within which we can make meaningful comparisons.

> ### It's the People, Stupid
> **Smart Managing**
> Gen-Xers did not throw out the concept of loyalty altogether. They transferred their natural affinity for loyalty from institutions to people. While a Boomer could be expected to "stick with the company" through thick and thin, the Gen-Xer is much more likely to "stick with the person." Hence the growing phenomenon of "teams" of workers moving from one organization to another en masse.

It's vital to realize that, although there are differences in attitudes and beliefs between Boomers or Gen-Xers, retaining top employees from either generation involves addressing the same principal issues. After all, people are people: no one flicked a switch in 1962 that changed everyone born after that date into a different species. The differences, as we shall see, are in the nature of the *response* by each generation, not in the issues themselves.

## The Seven Areas of Distinction in Employee Retention

Effective retention involves distinguishing how Boomers and Gen-Xers differ in their perceptions of the workplace, in particular the following seven areas:

- Work environment
- Work content
- Growth opportunities
- Compensation and rewards
- The organizational culture
- Work relationship with manager
- Work relationship with peers

Let's briefly summarize what we mean by each.

## Work Environment

Right at the core of Maslow's hierarchy of needs, work environment is a crucial factor in retention. For employees who stay with an organization for any length of time, the work environment (together with the organizational culture) is likely to be the biggest constant in their daily lives. Work content can change, compensation and benefits can change, relationships with peers can change, but for most people the "look and feel" of the physical space in which they work will remain pretty much the same.

Issues such as dress code, the ability to "individualize" their working environment, and even the physical location of their workspace vary from one demographic group to another, but at heart, for everyone, the issue is the ability to work in a pleasant environment.

## Work Content

First or second in practically every poll or survey on retention issues for top employees is the content of the work itself—that is, assignments or projects and associated performance goals.

Particularly for top employees, who have a reasonable expectation that they were not hired to complete repetitive, uninspiring tasks, the planning of work content to satisfy personal and career aspirations is an essential element of any effective retention strategy. Whether Boomer, Gen-Xer, or anything else, top-performing employees have little patience for being stuck in what they perceive as "dead-end" jobs with assignments that are limited or—worse—unplanned and unstructured.

## Growth Opportunities

Employees become top performers by constantly striving to grow, both personally and in their careers. Career and personal *growth opportunities* are therefore essential for retaining top performers.

Although (as we'll see) Boomers and Gen-Xers differ as to which growth opportunities they most respond to, of the seven retention factors this is the one about which, in general, the two generations are most in agreement. All top employees agree: stagnate and you're dead. A top performer's résumé is built by demonstrating regular, quantum increases in skills and achievements. If your organization doesn't provide such opportunities, top employees will leave.

### Dust off Those Job Specifications Smart Managing

Providing top employees with challenging and fulfilling assignments starts with the job specification. If the description is limited in scope and lacks vision, the chances are that the assignments flowing from it are equally uninspiring.

Review the job specifications for your retention target group(s). Do they make *you* excited? Would you apply for these jobs? If not, get the appropriate people together and discuss how you can improve the job specifications to make them catalysts for challenging assignments.

## Compensation and Rewards

Generally speaking, the issue of compensation and other quantifiable rewards is overstated in most employee retention strategies. As we'll see in Chapter 5, although compensation and rewards *are* an important part of recognizing and fulfilling the needs of employees, their impact is binary:

- Get it wrong (pay people materially lower than the market average) and everything else you do will have little or no impact.
- Get it right (pay people appropriately) and you're just "in the game"—you still have to get all the other six elements right.

**Don't Get Fooled Again**

A misperception has developed that Gen-Xers have a hugely unrealistic perception of their worth in the marketplace. This misperception is a direct result of the excesses of the dot-com era.

It's not that Gen-Xers are unrealistic—they're as capable as anybody at working out median salary ranges—but that for a brief but well-publicized period of time some high-profile employers paid unrealistically high salaries to Gen X employees. The fact that the Gen-Xers happily took such salaries while they were available doesn't mean that everyone of a certain age now believes they're worth more than the marketplace will pay.

## The Organizational Culture

Every organization—irrespective of size, industry, or location—has its own culture. Organizational culture isn't just composed of grand things like vision, values, and a mission statement, but it's also (even more so) defined by "habits"—the ways in which the organization does things, how its members communicate and interact, and what's expected and accepted and what's not.

All employees (not just top performers) will naturally stay longer with an organization where the culture makes them feel at home, as opposed to a culture that's threatening, overpowering, or just plain "blah."

In smaller organizations, culture is easier to control, because it's almost certainly a direct reflection of the attitudes and beliefs of the founders. However, once an organization grows

**Small Is Beautiful**

Some organizations go to extremes to avoid developing a "big company" culture. *Inc. Magazine* (a "must read" for anyone dealing with retaining top employees in a small or medium-sized organization) regularly presents reports and case studies on founders who have stopped growing their companies for fear of losing an important cultural ethic.

Meanwhile, for the same reason, Tetra Pak, one of the world's largest packaging companies, refuses to let any one site become larger than 250 employees. It simply builds a new plant or campus when employment at one location gets too high.

beyond a certain size, the culture takes on a life of its own and can become a negative factor in retention.

## Work Relationship with Manager

The final two factors address an area where there's a very distinct difference between the expectations of Boomers and Gen-Xers—relationships in the workplace.

The first and most important relationship is that between the employee and you—his or her manager. In most polls and surveys, this relationship alternates with the issue of work content (see above) as the first or second most important factor in keeping a top performer.

### The 12 Gallup Workplace Statements

In 1997 the Gallup Organization defined a set of 12 statements that a motivated, satisfied employee would make about his or her work environment. Of these 12 statements, five are directly related to the employee-manager relationship:

1. I know what is expected of me at work.
2. I have the materials and equipment I need to do my work right.
3. At work, I have the opportunity to do what I do best every day.
4. In the last seven days, I have received recognition or praise for doing good work.
5. My supervisor, or someone at work, seems to care about me as a person.
6. There is someone at work who encourages my development.
7. At work, my opinions seem to count.
8. The mission or purpose of my company makes me feel my job is important.
9. My fellow employees are committed to doing quality work.
10. I have a best friend at work.
11. In the last six months, someone at work has talked to me about my progress.
12. This last year, I have had opportunities at work to learn and grow.

Marcus Buckingham, the Gallup consultant who worked on the 12 Gallup Workplace Statements, has since published two business best sellers based on the statements:

*First, Break All the Rules: What the World's Greatest Managers Do Differently* (Marcus Buckingham and Curt Coffman, Simon & Schuster, 1999)

*Now, Discover Your Strengths* (Marcus Buckingham and Donald O. Clifton, Free Press, 2001)

The impact of this relationship on employee retention is even more important for top performers than for other employees, because of the changing nature of the relationship itself. For a top performer, the manager is much more than just a supervisor doling out tasks and appraising performance. The top performer will see the manager as much more of a mentor and a coach than a supervisor, helping him or her with personal and career growth (see "Growth Opportunities," above) as well as managing his or her job responsibilities.

### Work Relationship with Peers

The last of the seven factors that impact employee retention of both Boomers and Gen-Xers is their relationship with their peers. Top employees are often competitive, which makes peer interaction crucial to their job satisfaction. Even though many (though not all) top employees are relatively self-contained socially, they still need to interact with similarly effective individuals for the challenges and to better develop their skills and knowledge.

## Effective Tools for Retaining Boomers

In most industries, the top performers are mostly from the Boomer generation, born between 1945 and 1962. Now in their 40s and 50s, they have reached the apex of their careers and have the experience and abilities to hold the highest positions. Consequently, and because many modern industries were shaped by the same generation, retention strategies tend to have an inherent bias toward Boomer values.

> **CAUTION!**
> ### Age Isn't Always Chronological
> Although we're defining demographic groups based on dates of birth, "Boomerism" is as much a state of mind as a matter of years. An individual born into a Boomer family well after 1962 might well have adopted the Boomer mindset.

Let's examine the implications of dealing with Boomers.

### Work Environment

Boomers tend to respond more to structured and hierarchical work environments than to loose, unregulated environments.

Common in Boomer-dominated organizations are offices rather than cubicles, a standardized (or at least minimal) dress code, assistants or secretaries to help with administrative tasks, allocated parking spaces, nameplates on doors and desks, and regulated break and lunch policies. Boomer top employees will expect their

> **The IBM Way**
> The culture of IBM (International Business Machines) in the late '60s and early '70s exemplifies the Boomer work environment—white shirt, dark suit, blue tie, and every step seemingly dictated by company policy. Today such a highly regulated work environment seems antiquated, even slightly repressive, but it epitomizes the essence of the more authority-based, institutional Boomer mindset.

status and authority to be demonstrable and expect to receive a structured improvement in both as a result of high performance.

## Work Content

The most distinctive difference between Boomer and Gen X attitudes toward work content is time span. A Boomer-based organization will often think and plan quite happily in annual or even five-year cycles. In fact, for many Boomers the concept of a work assignment defaults to that of a *project*—a structured, planned series of activities, with allocated resources and responsibilities.

Boomers expect and thrive in environments where the work content is well planned, with clear goals and objectives and clear associated outcomes and rewards. To many Boomers, work assignments that seem thrown together on the fly, unstructured, unclear, or ambiguous and tasks that come in short bursts, unconnected, with little strategic overview, smack of superficiality or incompetence.

## Growth Opportunities

For a Boomer, growth and developmental opportunities are something to be earned—rewards, in a sense, for work done "in the trenches." Prevalent among Boomers is a utilitarian sense of "getting the primary job done first" before indulging in the more

> ### Smart Managing
> ## The Proof Is in the Pudding
> Review the most prominent personal and career development opportunities your organization provides—temporary assignments, extracurricular studies, sabbaticals, study assistance, and so on. What is the rate at which members of your target retention group take advantage of these opportunities? If the rate is less than 25% of the employees, then the opportunities you're providing are unattractive, unattainable, or both.

personal (less institutional) indulgence of personal and career growth.

Nevertheless, a Boomer top performer will fully expect that such opportunities be available and clearly achievable—and that the basis of attaining such opportunities be spelled out very clearly. An ambiguous or clearly unrealizable process for accessing personal and career growth opportunities will lead to frustration and an eventual parting of the ways.

## Compensation and Rewards

The type of compensation structure with which Boomers have grown up and (by and large) are more comfortable includes packages that are:

- standardized
- structured (tiered)
- linked to the position in the organization (i.e. "ranked")
- risk-averse—a relatively high base salary and a bonus or discretionary element corresponding to at most 30% or so of the total expected gross pay

Boomers tend to see compensation as a *reward* mechanism rather than a *motivational* tool. It's more consistent with the Boomer worldview that compensation is an expected return for the work they've committed to perform and that little should put that return at risk. At the extremes, a hugely disproportionate bonus element in a compensation package will cause Boomers to experience the same feelings about the management team as superficial and incompetent as an unstructured, "seat-of-the-pants" work schedule.

## The Organizational Culture

As we've already seen, Boomers are much more likely than Gen-Xers to develop a commitment to the organization and its goals. Consequently, Boomers respond best in environments where the organizational culture is clearly expressed and where that culture is regularly and consistently reinforced.

Senior managers will most inspire Boomer top performers by "walking the talk" and standing shoulder to shoulder with each other and with the organizational ethos.

"Maverick" cultures or a poorly communicated set of values make Boomers uneasy and unresponsive. Similarly, Boomers view internal carping or cynicism on an organizational level as disloyal and disruptive. (But on a personal level, Boomers can be just as carping or cynical as anyone else.)

## Work Relationship with Manager

Boomers grew up with a more pronounced sense of community than today's generation. Boomers were less likely to be part of a two-earner household than Gen-Xers and experienced less enforced mobility as a result of frequent parental job changes. Consequently, their roots in the community are stronger and their sense of communal interaction is more pronounced. (As an aside, since Boomers on average stayed longer in one place as children, they developed a stronger awareness of local authority figures.)

### The Organization Man

To fully understand the interaction between Boomers and organizational culture, the best resource is *The Organization Man* by William Hollingsworth Whyte. Published in 1956, this book explains how organizational culture was shaped by the post-WW II environment and how this in turn shaped the attitudes of the "Organization Man" of the 1950s, who shaped the workplace that Boomers began to enter in the 1960s.

Similarly prophetic in 1970 (and still so today) is *Up the Organization: How to Stop the Corporation from Stifling People and Strangling Profits* by Robert Townsend (ex-CEO of Avis Rent-A-Car). This slim but incisive book shows how corporate culture shaped the Boomer generation.

Boomer relationships with their managers tend as a result to be somewhat "easier" (in the social sense)—less prickly or confrontational than relationships between Gen-Xers and their managers. On the other hand, Boomers (as we've already seen) expect leadership, guidance, and authority from their managers. They typically deem it important that their managers act as a role model; even when top performers have moved beyond the need for role modeling from their managers, they will still expect it from them as an outworking of the corporate culture.

## Work Relationship with Peers

The same factors impact the Boomer relationship with their peers. A Boomer is more likely to have a strong overlap between business colleagues and "buddies" than Gen-Xers, who more typically have several categories of friends, with little overlap.

Boomers also have a stronger inherent commitment to team work and therefore tend to work together more naturally, pooling resources and ideas. Indeed, in an environment that doesn't provide such an opportunity of collaboration (preferably face to face—this is not the Internet generation) Boomer top employees will feel alienated and uncomfortable.

### Virtual Working

A good example of the Boomer attitude in work relationships with peers is the pendulum effect in recent years of the move to virtual working—working for an organization, but from home or a home office or permanently on the road.

Although employees of all ages originally embraced virtual working as a freeing, empowering concept, many Boomers have in recent years returned to the more classic work environment, largely because they've realized that the asocial nature of virtual working doesn't suit their personal needs.

Contrast this with the Gen X employees who have probably already spent half their adult life alone in front of a computer screen and for whom virtual working is a perfectly natural activity. For them, going into work every day and working face to face with team members is much more unnatural.

## Effective Tools for Retaining Gen-Xers

For any organization more than a couple of years old, providing for the needs of Boomers is less of a cultural shock than providing for the wave of Gen-Xers hitting the workplace. With 1963 as the arbitrary beginning of Generation X, many of that generation are now approaching their late 30s—time enough for many of them already to have emerged as top employees. Indeed, in some industries (fashion, some areas of entertainment, sports) they already dominate. The next 20 years will see them move into controlling positions everywhere. How must your organization change to accommodate that shift?

### Work Environment

In contrast with Boomers, Gen-Xers require their work environment to be much more an expression of *them*—their individuality, their attitudes, their interests and passions. Working in an environment that dictates an expression of the *organization's* values and achievements is much less motivating for Gen-Xers than for Boomers.

> **It Works the Other Way, Too** **CAUTION!**
>
> If you work for a Gen X organization, don't think you're exempt from demographic troubles! It's just as important for the Gen X organization to understand the Boomer mindset as the other way around. Even if you're never going to employ a Boomer (highly unlikely), your advisors, customers and clients, suppliers, investors, and industry opinion-formers probably are largely Boomers. You need to understand their mindset in order for your Gen X top performers to be able to interact with them positively and effectively.

Despite an apparent "couldn't care less" attitude to material things, Gen-Xers have a highly developed need to express themselves in the way they dress, the way they decorate their workspace, and the way they structure their day. Conversely, they have a less pronounced need for overt expressions of status: a Gen X top performer will often be happier hot-desking in a highly personalized open office space than occupying a corner office that feels soulless to him. To adapt for the oncoming

Gen X top performer, the organization must relax dress codes, decorative style, and standardized working environments.

### Work Content

Gen-Xers not only cope better than Boomers with short-burst, ambiguous, unclear assignments—they actually thrive on them. They're called the "MTV generation"—a label that may be unfair and sweeping, but expresses an underlying truth: Gen-Xers are much more able to work on a series of fast, unstructured tasks—even tasks without any apparent strategic sense of direction—without getting frustrated or suffering a loss of motivation.

**Flex from the Start**  Show flexibility in the working environment with your first interaction with Gen X top employees—the job interview. Very few Gen-Xers will be impressed with a formal interview environment—the interviewer(s), the candidate, and a desk between them like a moat defending the interviewer's position. At the very least, interview Gen-Xers in a conference room, seated at a round table. It's even better if you can have the interview in a real working environment, maybe with flip charts and markers available.

What's important to Gen X employees is that the tasks be challenging and use their skills to the maximum possible. Give a Gen-Xer an unrewarding, mundane task and he or she will typically stay around for a lot shorter time than will the Boomer, who has a stronger underlying sense of loyalty to the organization.

For the Gen-Xer, the project is all—often to the exclusion of the organization. Give a Gen-Xer the choice between working for well-known Company A on a boring assignment or unknown Company B on a cutting-edge project and he or she is much more likely to choose the latter.

## Growth Opportunities

For Gen X employees, personal and career growth opportunities come with the territory: they must be built into the package right from the start. For Gen-Xers, the notion of having to tread water, to prove worthy before being allowed to benefit from personal growth opportunities, is alien.

This is, to some extent, a reflection of the differences in education opportunities afforded Boomers and Gen-Xers. Many Boomers were the first of their family to go to college and viewed that opportunity (and similar developmental opportunities later on in life) as a privilege. Gen-Xers, on the other hand, live at a time when college education is a much more accepted, natural part of growing up. Gen-Xers therefore *expect* to be trained, educated, and developed as part of their job—not as a reward for good performance.

## Compensation and Rewards

As with growth opportunities, Gen-Xers expect compensation packages to be based on performance—not on length of time served, apparent status, or any other systemic measurement. They want to be recognized and rewarded for what they

### Access, Not Content

**Smart Managing**

If you have a roster of personal and growth opportunities available for employees and if your employees are taking advantage of the opportunities at a reasonable rate (see "The Proof Is in the Pudding," p. 68), it's highly likely that you need do little to change the actual opportunities for Gen X employees. The main change will involve the *access* to such opportunities. You may well need to do away with such restrictions as tenure-based rules preventing access to paid study leave until someone has worked for the organization for X years.

Be aware that making these changes will almost certainly provoke negative reactions among employees who had to put in time waiting for such opportunities, but since you're improving the situation for all employees, such reactions will be short-lived. In any case, it's better to deal with a little dissatisfaction than to maintain the old system based on time served.

do, not just the position they hold or the length of time they've been with the organization. As a result, Gen-Xers typically are comfortable with a higher risk-reward element (bonuses and discretionary payments) in their compensation package than Boomers.

Here are some other factors that Gen-Xers appreciate:

- A combination of team-based and individual rewards reflecting the success of their team as well as their own individual work.
- Non-traditional, non-cash benefits, such as non-work retreats, sporting events, and free food and drinks.
- More frequent, smaller payouts (quarterly or even monthly, rather than the annual bonus that appeals to Boomers with their more structured, medium- to long-term view).

### The Organizational Culture

Gen-Xers are much less motivated by a monolithic, impersonal organizational structure (no matter how impressive) than by the answer to that age-old radio call sign, WII-FM—"What's in it for me?"

Unlike Boomers, who are more likely to appreciate the organization's values and ethos for their intrinsic importance, Gen-Xers need to feel that espoused values impact them directly.

The ways in which Gen-Xers look to the organizational culture to impact their lives may well change over the next few decades, but at this point these are the key expectations that Gen X employees have of your organizational culture:

> **⚠ CAUTION!**
> **What the Future May Bring**
> Gen-Xers are aging just like everyone else, so keep an eye on those non-cash benefits to see if Gen-X top employees continue to hold them in high regard. As Gen-Xers take on more responsibilities (and liabilities) and the impact of mortgages and children takes hold, it may well be that pension plans and cash bonuses will experience a resurgence in importance.

- **Work-life balance.** The holy grail of the 1990s, the elusive balance between achievement and social interaction
  still eludes many. Gen-Xers may be the worst generation
  yet at achieving such a balance, but they are also the
  most active defenders of the right to have it!
- **Acceptance of their views and opinions.** Many Gen-Xers
  saw their parents (probably their fathers, given the demo-
  graphics at the time) keep their thoughts to themselves
  and steadily work their way up the corporate ladder. Most
  Gen-Xers have been educated in an environment that
  eschews such an approach and encourages them to
  speak up—and they expect to be heard. An organizational culture that assumes that they'll stay quiet and pay
  their dues will not remain attractive for long.
- **Respect for the individual.** Gen X employees are often
  much more individualistic than their more team-oriented
  Boomer colleagues and predecessors. This difference can
  certainly challenge a manager: a group of individualistic
  superstars is no guarantee of easy success—ask the
  coach of any sports team! And the Gen-Xer will not toler-
  ate an organizational culture that emphasizes the team to
  the total exclusion of the individual.

### Work Relationship with Manager

The socially independent, more mobile Gen-Xer has less need than the Boomer to feel that his or her man-ager is a "buddy." Yet there's a higher demand from Gen-Xers for mentor-ing and coaching as a managerial skill than at any time previously. The

> **The Army Gets It**
>
> It's interesting that even the U.S. Army—an organization emphasizing teamwork, if ever there was one—has felt a need to shape its recruiting activities to recognize the individual. Faced with a rapidly drop-ping recruitment rate, in the late '90s it launched its recruiting drive with a new slogan, "An Army of One."

reason for this stems from two of the factors already mentioned

---

### Prepare Yourself!

**Smart Managing**   The expectation of Gen-Xers that their managers should mentor and coach them has caused a crisis of confidence in managers in recent years. The enormous growth in training in mentoring and coaching skills is a direct response to this demand. Many managers feel threatened by what seems to them to be a change in the rules of the game.

To prepare for an increase in Gen X employees, first prepare yourself!

Develop your mentoring and coaching skills. Don't wait until the demand is there and the skills are needed immediately: nothing makes learning a new skill more difficult than doing it under such pressure.

We'll examine the role of the manager in retaining top employees in Chapters 9 and 10 and the role of mentoring and coaching in Chapter 11.

---

above—a belief that personal and career growth should be a given, not an earned bonus, and a desire for their views and opinions to be heard and taken into account. Gen-Xers look to their manager for both—and top performers, in particular, will not be satisfied with less.

Conversely, Gen-Xers do *not* react well to being micro-managed by their bosses. Unlike Boomers, who will expect a degree of oversight from their managers, Gen-Xers respond poorly to the supervisory aspect of managing. They expect their managers to trust them to do the job and then judge them by the results, rather than to herd them toward a desired outcome. (This is not to say that such an attitude is always reasonable or correct, but merely to point out that Gen-Xers can experience difficulty with the authoritative aspects of management while responding well to mentoring and coaching.)

### Work Relationship with Peers

With the increase of Gen-Xers in the workplace, appreciation has grown for the potential of *peer* relationships—peer mentoring, peer coaching, peer review groups, peer quality control.

Boomers have a pyramidal, top-down, command-and-control mindset. Gen-Xers think laterally and, when faced with a problem, are more likely to seek an answer within their peer group than to seek clarification "from above."

Smart organizations have recognized and benefited from this sense of autonomy that's inherent in Gen-Xers. When you encourage Gen X employees to pursue their natural, lateral leaning, they can act effectively as self-supervisors for each other. This allows you to lighten the burden of routine chores of day-to-day management from the manager-employee relationship, so you can interact with the employees on a more strategic level.

## Wassup? Planning for Retaining Gen-Yers

There's yet another generation on the way!

People born after 1982 (currently called Generation Y) are already working in your friendly neighborhood fast-food joint and are beginning to enter the mainstream workforce. We may well see the very first top employees from this generation emerge over the next two or three years in industries such as high tech, entertainment, and sports, where youth is a distinct advantage.

With internships and weekend jobs already behind them, Gen-Yers have their own clear expectations for their employers and, although it may be too early to tell what they'll be like as top performers, here are a few "thought prompters" about Gen-Yers:

> **Retaining Generation Y**
>
> If you need to start planning to retain Gen-Yers right away, then get the latest book in an excellent series: *Managing Generation Y* by Carolyn A. Martin and Bruce Tulgan (HRD Press, 2001), available from www.amazon.com or rainmakerthinking.com.

- They're typically more upbeat and optimistic than Gen-Xers.
- They're more at ease than Gen-Xers with other age groups.
- They've reinvented their own version of loyalty (a concept held by the Boomers, but rejected by Gen-Xers), but to different institutions than before.
- They're the most globalized generation to date.

- This is the generation of the hyperlink: their thought processes are synaptic, not linear.

## Manager's Checklist for Chapter 4

❏ Most jobs in the workplace are currently held by Baby Boomers or members of Generation X.

❏ Most top employees are currently Boomers, but the next wave will be from Generation X.

❏ People are people, whatever their generation, and each individual must be treated with consideration and respect.

❏ It's easy to be glib and superficial about the differences among the generations.

❏ Boomers and Gen-Xers have different perceptions and expectations of the workplace.

❏ Some organizations are already preparing for the *next* generation of top employees—Generation Y.

# Compensation: Why It (Almost) Doesn't Matter

*We're overpaying him, but he's worth it.*
—Samuel Goldwyn

*A reward cannot be valued if it is not understood.*
—Philip C. Grant

For many organizations, the entire concept of retaining top employees boils down to one topic—compensation. "To keep our best employees, we must pay them well" is the cry. Well, up to a point, that's true—but only as a negative. If you *don't* pay your top performers well, they'll surely leave. But *only* paying them well does not ensure that they'll stay.

In this chapter we'll examine the role of compensation in retaining top employees and show how a well-designed compensation plan *can* be important in retaining your top employees—so long as it's designed properly and in conjunction with the rest of your retention strategy.

## Why Compensation (Almost) Doesn't Matter

Why doesn't simply paying well solve the retention problem? For two reasons.

As any good salesperson will tell you, a sale on the basis of price alone is the worst kind of sale—it establishes no buyer-seller relationship, beyond that of price, and as soon as someone offers a better price, your customer is gone. It's the same with the employer-employee relationship. Establishing that relationship on the basis of compensation alone turns your employee into a mercenary for hire: the next organization to come along with a better offer will prove a more attractive proposition.

Compensation is essentially a *satisfier*, not a *motivator*. Adjusting it has a one-time, temporary effect on the employee—not a long-term, sustained effect.

### Satisfiers Versus Motivators

Frederick Herzberg's satisfier or hygiene theory states that there are certain things that make employees unhappy by their absence, but that, once present, lose their motivational effect.

Here's a simple example. It's a sweltering afternoon; the employees are hot. The boss decides to go out and buy everyone an ice cream. Production rises. Thrilled with the result, the next afternoon, he buys *two* ice creams apiece. Will production double again? What if he buys three ice creams for each employee? 10? 100? The ice cream is a satisfier. It has a one-

**Key Term**

**Satisfier** Factor that is necessary to prevent job dissatisfaction. Also called *hygiene factor.*

**Motivator** Factor that causes job satisfaction.

These terms come from Frederick Herzberg, the researcher mentioned in Chapter 1. Herzberg showed that satisfaction and dissatisfaction at work nearly always were the result of *different* factors, not simply opposite reactions to the same factors.

In the Herzberg model, satisfaction is the result of *motivators* like opportunity for advancement, recognition, responsibility, advancement, etc., and dissatisfaction resulted from *satisfiers* or *hygiene factors* such as physical work environment, company policies, and salary.

time positive impact on production; providing ever greater amounts does not multiply the production gains accordingly.

Compensation is the same. Remove it (or reduce it below reasonable expectations) and everyone is unhappy. Put it in place and it's time to move on to other matters— there's only so much return to be gained from increasing compensation.

**Millionaire Salespeople**

Herzberg's theory is at play every day in the world of sales. In theory, any good salesperson with an open-ended commission package and a reasonable product should be a millionaire. Just sell, sell, sell! But every rep has a level at which the compensation satisfies the demand on his or her time and energies and it eventually becomes more attractive to stop selling and return to home and family.

## Compensation Creates a One-Time Adjustment

If your compensation policies are below market level (we'll get to that point later in this chapter), you'll have trouble retaining top employees because you're not meeting their compensation needs. If you adjust compensation upward to meet the market level, you get a one-time effect on employee retention. But this is where many organizations make the mistake of stopping their retention efforts. In fact, stopping at this point usually makes employee turnover worse in the long run, because of the "weed garden" effect outlined in Chapter 1 (p. 10).

## Compensation Must Be Part of the Retention Mix

Avoiding the "weed garden" effect involves placing the compensation plan for your top performers in the context of an overall retention strategy. You can do this in two ways:

1. Construct the compensation plan to connect with the other elements of your retention strategy. For example, you might design an incentive element to be paid on the successful completion of the organization's orientation program (which you'll design in Chapter 8) or on the satisfactory conclusion of a mentoring or coaching relationship (see Chapter 11).

2. Construct other elements of your retention strategy to take over from your compensation plan as motivators. For example, a top sales performer might receive a cash bonus for some years on attaining certain goals, but in year three she might instead be made eligible for inclusion in the organization's management succession plan.

### Baton Race

**Smart Managing**  Think of compensation as the fast runner who takes the first leg in a baton race. Just like that first runner, whose goal is to open up a lead that competitors can't overcome, compensation can make an immediate impact on the retention of your top employees, establishing a lead that then passes to the other elements of your retention strategy. Just don't try to make the lead runner run the whole race!

## What a Compensation Plan Must Achieve

Now that we've discussed how compensation, for maximum effect, must be used in context with your overall retention strategy, let's examine what your compensation package must achieve. What are your compensation goals?

### The Key Objective of Compensation Is Not Just Performance

In the "status quo" employer-employee relationship (Chapter 1), when the deal was "You come work for me, do a good job, and, so long as economic conditions allow, I will continue to employ you," the key role of compensation was to *enhance performance*.

### Set Clear Goals

**MISTAKE PROOFING**  In my experience, most organizations don't adequately address setting clear *retention* goals for a compensation package. As a result, managers end up making one-time "deals" with each individual, a situation that leads to a complicated, unworkable amalgam of inconsistent practices. Also, such deals tend to come when the top performer has already expressed a desire to go elsewhere—and agreeing on compensation under such terms brings us right back to the problem of dealing on price discussed at the start of this chapter.

Clarify the retention goals of your compensation package in advance and avoid a lot of confusion down the line.

---

**Examine Annual Reviews**

TRICKS OF THE TRADE

A good way to see if your compensation package is adequately addressing both performance and retention is to examine the content of your top employees' annual reviews (or whatever time frame you use). Is the discussion equally about performance and retention (past and future) or is it more about one at the expense of the other? If there's an untoward bias toward either past performance or future rewards, then your compensation package is inadequately balanced. Your compensation package should be designed in such a way as to ensure that both the employees and their managers are equally concerned about past performance and future rewards.

---

In the absence of job mobility, so long as the employee was being paid reasonably in line with the market, he or she was likely to stay with the employer indefinitely. So retention was not an issue—and certainly not a compensation issue. Compensation was all about *performance*.

Some organizations still think that way. Their compensation policies are designed primarily with performance in mind; adjustments to address retention are "bolted on" later (see sidebar). The result is often a Frankenstein-like amalgamation of incentives, bonuses, base pay, and perks that resembles in its muddled complexity an amateur attempt at electrical wiring.

Compensation is no longer about performance alone. It's now about performance *and* retention. You must build in both objectives right from the start.

### Setting Your Retention-Related Compensation Goals

This book is not the place to discuss the classic, performance-based goals of your compensation policies. (For that I strongly recommend *Recognizing and Rewarding Employees*, by R. Brayton Bowen, McGraw-Hill, 2000.) Here we'll concentrate on setting *retention-related* goals.

(Of course, we shall see that—especially for top employees—performance and retention are connected in a number of ways. We'll look at an example in the next section. But setting operational performance goals—"How many blue widgets should Joe sell this year?"—is outside the scope of this book.)

## Compensation as Recognition

Top performers want to know (and usually want others to know) that they've delivered the goods.

The first retention goal of the compensation package should be to provide the tools to allow the employees to clearly establish whether or not they've achieved their goals for the period under review.

There's nothing more frustrating for top employees than to be unsure if they're making the grade or not. If the confusion and frustration about this point lasts, the employees usually leave.

It's vital, then, that your compensation packages leave no room for doubt as to whether the employees have met targets or not and what the implications are either way.

**Let Others Know, Too**
Remember: there's a fair amount of ego involved in being a top employee. Consider making performance recognition a matter of public record.

When I owned the Pizza Hut franchise in Ireland, I would circulate the discretionary bonuses paid to the top 10 unit managers each quarter. The public recognition not only affected performance by generating a sense of competition, but it also helped us keep many of our best managers in a very competitive market.

## Compensation as Motivation

Top employees need motivation—it's what gets them up in the morning. If they don't feel motivated, they'll eventually move on.

So as well as recognition, your compensation package must include motivational elements—incentives, bonuses, and perks that motivate employees not just occasionally, but regularly. Many organizations resort to motivational compensation too late—when the employees' morale has already dropped. ("Things are looking ugly out there. We better throw them a bonus.") This is almost always a dollar short and a day late. Build motivational elements into your compensation package right from the start.

## Compensation as a Team-Builder

Top employees can be notoriously poor as team members. Although this isn't true of all top performers, many consider

**This Isn't Just for Sales**

*Smart Managing*

Motivational compensation elements are usually easiest to construct for salespeople: they usually have clear targets and the motivational rewards are based on attaining those goals. Smart managers establish motivational elements for *all* their top employees. It may seem harder to establish motivational rewards for the head of the audit team in the accounts department, for example, but with the tools presented later in this chapter you should be able to construct a set of motivational rewards to match his position.

And if you're unsure about what motivational elements to include in designing a compensation package, you have the perfect focus group—your employees.

their success to be the result of their own efforts alone.

One result of this is an adverse effect on retention. Top employees can suffer (at their own hands) from a lack of assimilation into the wider group. This is one reason why the maverick overachiever often moves from job to job.

Your compensation package for top performers should include team-based rewards that reflect the achievement of the group and encourage the employees to interact with others to achieve mutually desirable goals. Although this won't solve the "assimilation problem" for everyone (inveterate mavericks will just ignore this aspect of their compensation altogether and focus on the individual rewards), it will push the borderline cases into more effective teamwork and, hence, a longer stay.

## Compensation as a Form of Accountability

Some top employees are not very teachable. It's perhaps understandable that employees who've achieved the status of top performers will feel that there's little they can be taught about how to do their job. While this may be true with regard to their core skills (and even there it's unlikely that they cannot learn more), this attitude can be dangerous when it comes to understanding the organization's wider goals and being accountable for working toward them.

Top employees have a tendency often to focus on their own "turf" to the exclusion of everything else and to wave off attempts to get them to see the bigger picture. A world-class research scientist or software programmer, for example, will often plead to be left alone to do their work and will beg off meetings concerning anything they view as "unimportant" (usually anything to do with leadership, finances, setting goals, or planning projects).

This has the same effect on retention as the previous issue regarding teamwork. By not being connected to the "core" of the organization—by being only semi-connected, if you will—the top employee is vulnerable from a retention point of view. (Usually in this case, the employee awakes as from a dream to find that the evil employer has completely abandoned the laissez-faire cultural ethos that first prompted the person to join the organization and is pressing too hard for him to conform to financial and other areas of accountability. Suddenly, he's off, usually leaving bad feelings.)

In this situation, your compensation package must include a strong level of accountability from the outset. Whether you attribute an element of payment to submitting regular reports or attending specific meetings or helping attain wider organizational goals (such as building the skills of the team), the clearer you make such goals at the outset, the better your chances of increasing accountability.

---

**TRICKS OF THE TRADE**

**Use Base Compensation, Not Incentives**

To effectively promote accountability, this element of a top employee's compensation package must be based on withholding a part of the base compensation against compliance with the relevant issues, not on paying an incentive or giving perks for compliance. Die-hard "non-accountables" will just ignore the incentives and perks and continue to remain semi-detached.

---

## Compensation as a Trust-Builder

One of the most positive factors in retaining top performers is the development of trust between the employer and the employee. That trust is expressed most acutely in the compensation package and how it's administered.

To use your compensation package to build trust, it must be built on four pillars. It must be:

1. Fair
2. Clear
3. Consistent
4. Honored

It is harder to fulfill these four requirements than it seems, because changes in circumstances can place some of these characteristics in conflict with others.

Here's an example. You've set up compensation packages for your salespeople. Then, if a new line of products is introduced, you may need to change the payment terms of commissions to reflect this. You're being fair, certainly, but maybe the payment schedule becomes overly complex and therefore unclear. To simplify the schedule, you introduce a few more changes in wording, some of which work and some don't. Before you know it, although you've acted with the best of intentions, some employees feel that you're not being consistent in the way you are paying them. The next thing you know, while you're trying to get your commission definitions right, a month slips by without payments, because no one is quite sure on what basis to make the payments. Result? A breach in the trust between you and your employees.

**Pick Your Issue**

In my experience, most organizations are consistently weak on *one* of the four pillars, not on all four. In that case, don't try to redesign your compensation policies from scratch around all four pillars. You can improve them considerably by concentrating on just *one aspect*.

It's worth polling your employees to get their perception on the area where the policies are weakest. Ask them to indicate whether they feel you can make the most improvement in being fair, clear, or consistent in your policies or simply in honoring the compensation agreement. Then, work on that one pillar.

## What to Include in Your Compensation Plan

Having established the retention-related goals of your compensation package, let's now look at the individual elements of the compensation package that you'll use to achieve those goals.

All compensation elements come under one of six main headings:

1. Base pay
2. Incentives
3. Bonuses
4. Deferred compensation (including stock options)
5. Benefits
6. Perks

We'll examine each category in turn, looking at the main ways in which you can use it to attain your retention goals.

### Base Pay

Base pay is the fixed element of compensation, paid in cash, usually monthly or biweekly. From a retention perspective, as we've already seen, base pay is the most fundamental of satisfiers: it causes grief if it's not there or it's less than the employee believes to be fair market value, but it contributes little to retention.

It should be your goal to use the tools later in this chapter to regularly review base pay in your compensation packages (say twice a year), to keep it at or near market value.

**Key Term — Market value** The average compensation an employee could get elsewhere for performing the same task. Later in this chapter, we'll consider some tools for establishing market value for your major job categories.

As we've seen, you can reserve some element of base pay to help develop accountability in top employees, if necessary. (See pp. 85-86 for more details.) Similarly, while the consistent and regular payment of base pay does not in itself build trust in the employee (another retention-related compensation goal), *failure* to pay it—even once—will enormously undermine any trust that you've built.

## Incentives

Incentives are elements of compensation paid to employees who attain goals that the employer and the employees reasonably expect can be attained in the period under review. Incentives may be cash or nonrecurring, non-cash benefits (e.g. extra vacation time, a paid holiday or conference, gift vouchers, etc.). For reasons detailed below, incentives are most often cash.

Because employees view the incentive targets as being attainable, over time they usually come to see incentives almost as a part of base pay (unlike bonuses, as explained in the next section).

As with base pay, the real room for damage with incentives is that failure to pay them will damage or destroy the employees' trust. (That's true for almost any reason. If an employee fails to meet the targets, he or she will lose trust in the employer's ability to set targets that are attainable. If an employee meets the targets, but the employer just doesn't want to pay out, the employee will lose trust in the employer's basic honesty. The only case in which the employer gets a break is if the employee fails to make the targets *and* accepts responsibility for failing.)

It's essential, therefore, that incentive goals be set clearly and transparently and that any failure to pay the incentives be mutually understood as being for fair and logical reasons. For top employees especially, any sense that the employer is "massaging" results to avoid paying incentives or is setting incentive targets artificially high will lead to major retention problems.

Incentives look like they should motivate (one

**Watch Your Reputation**

The area of unmet incentive targets is fraught with difficulty for an employer's reputation. Fudging incentive targets or manipulating results to avoid paying out will severely damage your chances of hiring top performers. Don't do it!

Even the perception of doing so can cause damage. So if you do not pay an incentive that the employee could reasonably expect was earned, make sure that you discuss the issue and reach a common understanding about the reason(s) for the nonpayment.

of our retention-related goals), both by their nature and by the creativity in the types of incentives. However, as we've seen, because the targets should be attainable, most top employees view incentives almost as part of base pay and, as a result, will probably be counting on receiving them. (In fact, some will have spent their incentives long before they've earned them!) For this reason, be careful about switching a cash-based incentive into a non-cash incentive—your employees may not like it.

### Bonuses

Bonuses, in contrast with incentives, are something that employees could not reasonably expect to attain in the normal course of events. Bonuses can be either *prospective* or *reactive*:

- **Prospective:** A bonus that will be paid if the employee attains a "stretch target"—a goal that's beyond what the employee could reasonably achieve.
- **Reactive:** A bonus that the organization decides to pay after the employee has achieved something out of the ordinary that was not planned (like landing a big new account or discovering a new process that will save major costs).

As with incentives, bonuses can be paid either in cash or as a nonrecurring, non-cash benefit (e.g. extra vacation time, a paid holiday or conference, gift vouchers, etc.). However,

**Smart Managing**

### Making the Most of Bonuses

Well-designed and -implemented bonus plans can do several things to help you meet your compensation retention goals.

Imagine that the VP of R&D tells the head of the team of R&D scientists that if, in addition to meeting their normal operational goals for the year, they additionally bring one entirely new product into beta testing by the end of the year, fully documented in accordance with company policies, then as a bonus the company will send the entire team to Hawaii for a week—all expenses paid plus extra time off. They achieve that goal and earn the bonus. If this achievement is properly communicated, it's a source of public recognition for the employees, a motivating factor, a team-building exercise, a lesson in accountability, and a trust builder, all at the same time.

bonuses are unlike incentives in that the employee does *not* reasonably anticipate a bonus in advance and the employer can therefore give them in forms other than cash more easily than incentives.

## Deferred Compensation

Under this heading comes any compensation that is earned but not paid until some time in the future—the most common of which is the stock option. Stock options in particular were, for a brief time during the dot-com boom, heralded as the panacea for all retention ills: just give the employees some stock options that don't vest until some years down the line and ... voilà! The retention problem is solved.

Unfortunately, it's not as simple as that. In fact, the end result can often be just the opposite. At the extreme, stock options can have a *negative* retention effect. Awarding stock options with a vesting date in the future simply sets a time for some employees to leave—the vesting date or shortly thereafter. The reason for this is simple: with the options held out before them, those employees consider every little bump or hollow in the employer-employee relationship as something to endure in order to make it to the vesting date.

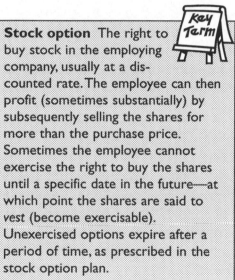

**Stock option** The right to buy stock in the employing company, usually at a discounted rate. The employee can then profit (sometimes substantially) by subsequently selling the shares for more than the purchase price. Sometimes the employee cannot exercise the right to buy the shares until a specific date in the future—at which point the shares are said to vest (become exercisable). Unexercised options expire after a period of time, as prescribed in the stock option plan.

Instead of maturely discussing workplace issues and resolving them, the employees adopt a "martyr" stance and wait out the time until they can leave, options in hand.

Does this mean that deferred compensation plans, and particularly stock options, have no place in your compensation package? Not at all. They play an important role—but it's important to be clear about that role.

Deferred compensation does not of itself promote employee retention by simply forcing the employee to wait around until the deferred compensation is paid or the stock options vest. It *will* positively impact retention if you use it to meet any or all of our retention-related compensation goals:

1. Recognition
2. Motivation
3. Team building
4. Accountability
5. Trust-building

Design your deferred compensation to serve as a form of recognition, certainly (by publicly announcing the award, for example), and to motivate employees to want to earn their stock options. Build in team-building or accountability requirements for employees to qualify for deferred compensation. Build trust by consistently making payments. But don't just award a deferred compensation package with a date three years in the future and assume that you've successfully "locked in" your top employees.

## Benefits

Benefits are recurring non-cash rewards that are deemed to be part of base pay. A health plan, dental payments, vacation, pension, life insurance coverage, a car—all of these are bene-fits. In fact, the list is limited only by the imagination of the employee or the employer!

For most jobs there's a mix of benefits that the

### Influence Equals Impact

**Smart Managing** As a general rule, the more an individual can influence the value of his or her deferred compensation, the more effect it has as a motivator. A CEO, who can directly affect the company's share price by her acts, is more likely to be motivated by stock options than an employee some distance away from strategic decision-making. In fact, if you award stock options to an employee who has absolutely no sense of being able to influence the stock value, you can engender a feeling of helplessness and accelerate the "martyr syndrome" described earlier.

employee views as part of his or her base pay. This mix is usually the result of market practices, the organizational culture, and tradition. As a result, the same considerations apply to these benefits as to base pay: they are satisfiers, so the employee will be upset if you don't provide them or you reduce them, but they contribute little to retention.

**Don't Take Benefits Lightly**

It's amazing how often employers miss the fact that employees view benefits as an element of their base pay. When times are tight, employers often put employee benefits high on the list of costs to be cut—and are often stunned at the vehemence of the employee response. This is usually because the employer has failed to make the distinction between *benefits* and *perks*.

## Perks

Perks (perquisites) are non-cash rewards that are *not* deemed to be part of base pay. Perks can be recurring—such as fitness clubs, on-site child care, subscriptions, and memberships of various sorts—or nonrecurring—such as computer equipment for personal use, tickets for sporting or entertainment events, and even free massages.

Perks are to benefits what bonuses are to incentives: they're much more effective than benefits for retention. Employees *expect* benefits; they *appreciate* perks. So (as with bonuses), do everything you can to maximize the retention effect of perks. They must meet the "four pillar" test:

**Keep Perks as Perks**

A perk given once is a perk. A perk given twice is a benefit. A perk given a third time is a right! Perks, which should be seen as above and beyond what might be expected in the compensation package, have a tendency to congeal into benefits—something employees view as a part of their base pay. Use the tips at the end of this chapter to make sure your perks retain their "perk status" and don't end up becoming benefits.

- They must be used for public recognition. (One CEO I know lets the "employee of the month" use her

Ferrari for one week—pretty good public recognition with that perk!)

- They must be motivational. (A Ferrari for a week might not thrill everyone. Match your perks to your employees.)
- They must involve team building and accountability to qualify (if these are issues with your better employees).
- They must build trust among the employees. (Don't position company freebies like T-shirts and mugs as perks or try to pass off unwanted gifts or airline miles that can be redeemed only between 4 p.m. and 5 p.m. two days a year. For top employees in particular, such gestures will have a negative effect on trust.)

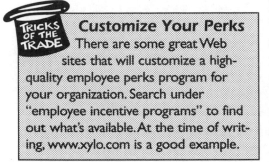

**Customize Your Perks**
There are some great Web sites that will customize a high-quality employee perks program for your organization. Search under "employee incentive programs" to find out what's available. At the time of writing, www.xylo.com is a good example.

## How to Design Your Compensation Plan

After you've established the retention-related goals and the reward categories for your compensation package, the next step is to design the package itself. In this section we'll look at how to gather the data you require to design your plan.

### Perform an Internal Audit

The first thing to do is to audit the current compensation situation. This is often an eye-opening exercise!

There are four sources for the information you require:

- **Consult personnel records.** These will show what each employee is receiving by way of compensation. You should view this information only as a starting point.
- **Check the last performance appraisal and/or periodic review.** You may well find that some adjustments you made to the employee's compensation package haven't yet reached personnel documentation, particularly if

they're in the form of incentives or bonuses not yet
earned. (Base pay and benefits adjustments are usually
reflected in personnel records fairly quickly.)

- **Refresh your own memory.** There may well be other
adjustments or perks that you gave at your discretion
since the last performance or periodic review that aren't
yet documented anywhere at all!

- **Discuss with the employee.** You might find that an
employee misunderstands some aspect of the compensation package (particularly perks). For example, one
year I had a spare set of season tickets for the local
orchestra and I casually gave them to a particularly valued employee. The next year we had an embarrassing
moment when he came by my office to pick up his set
of tickets for the current season.

## Surveys

Now you know what your organization is doing. The next step is
to find out how your compensation program compares with
what other organizations are doing.

This used to be an arduous, time-consuming task, but here,
once again, the Internet comes to the rescue. Survey results on
compensation and rewards for just about every job description
under the sun are available at the click of a mouse. Web sites
come and go, so as always, use a search engine to find out
what's available right now. (Type "salary survey" into your
favorite search engine.) At the time of writing, these are
the three best resources:

- www.salary.com
- www.wageweb.com
- www.bls.gov/ncs/
(U.S. Bureau of
Labor Statistics
National
Compensation
Survey)

> **Making It Real** TRICKS OF THE TRADE
>
> Most compensation survey
> sites include "power search" functions
> that allow you to adjust for geograph-
> ic location and industry specializa-
> tions. Take time to learn and use
> these features. The little effort
> involved will more than pay off in the
> quality, accuracy, and relevance of the
> information you receive.

## Benchmarking

After gathering internal and external data, the next step is to compare both, to establish in what areas (if any) you need to make adjustments to bring your compensation plan up to the market level. I recommend making the comparison over the six reward categories detailed above:

1. Base pay
2. Incentives
3. Bonuses
4. Deferred compensation (including stock options)
5. Benefits
6. Perks

As a rule of thumb, if any element of your current compensation package is more than 15% below the industry standard (as shown by the survey results), you *must* make an adjustment, to remain competitive. If you are between 5% and 15% below the industry standard, you will need to make an adjustment only if other elements of the package do not in some way compensate. In other words, if your base pay is 10% lower than the industry average, but your bonuses and benefits are substantially more, you will probably not need to make an adjustment.

If you are out by 5% or less, you probably do not need to make any adjustment, except in the most competitive industries, but you *should* check back regularly (maybe every six months) to make sure the gap has not widened.

**Converting Apples to Oranges**

**Smart Managing** When comparing your compensation package with others, the cash elements are easiest to compare. Non-cash incentives, benefits, and perks are trickier. I usually multiply the annual cash value of the item by 3, to convert it to a cash amount for comparison purposes. So, a subscription to a fitness club costing $450 a year would convert to $1,350 (3 × $450) cash value.

## Testing and Feedback

This element of designing a compensation package is often overlooked. It's highly likely that some part of your newly designed compensation plan won't fly: some element will be too clunky, too hard to understand or impractical to administer. For example, a cleverly calculated incentive scheme may be so convoluted that no one is too sure just what should be paid, to whom, and when.

Use a confidential feedback mechanism, like a blind survey, to assess how the new plan is working. I recommend testing for validity at three months, six months, one year, and three years after implementation, then every three years thereafter.

## Maximizing the Results from Your Compensation Plan

How can you get the biggest bang for your compensation buck? Let's end this chapter with a few short tips on how to get the most retention value out of your carefully constructed compensation package.

> **Ask the Right Questions**
>
> Aim your surveys appropriately. The initial surveys (at three and six months) will evaluate the base pay and benefits and perhaps (depending on the timing of their payment) the incentives and perks. The annual survey will evaluate base pay, benefits, incentives, bonuses, and perks. The three-year survey will evaluate the effectiveness of all of the above plus deferred compensation.

### Communicate!

There's no point in having the best compensation plan in the business if no one knows about it! Your newly designed package should be part of your recruitment literature as well as broadcasted appropriately within the organization. Don't forget: top employees want recognition; your compensation package is one way of providing that recognition.

### Show That Compensation Is Fair and Appropriate

It's very important that the introduction of the new compensation plan be accompanied by a detailed explanation, one on one, to each of the employees affected by it, describing how the new plan will work and why it's fair and appropriate. You may wish to con-

**Appropriate Communication**

Only you can know what constitutes "appropriate communication" of compensation packages within your organization. Organizational attitudes vary from the completely secret to 100% transparent. In my experience, the more open the communication about compensation, the higher the retention. Secrecy breeds distrust and, as we've noted, distrust breeds turnover.

sider sharing with them the results of your benchmarking exercise. After all, these people will be most directly affected by the compensation plan and they deserve an individual explanation of its implications.

## Show Demonstrable Results

As you conduct the surveys detailed in the section above and compare the outcome of the new compensation plan against the targets you've set, share the results with all of your employees. If your new plan has resulted in a 13% increase in sales or the launch of a new product, tell everyone. Success is great for retaining employees!

### Deal with Both Risk and Reward

For your compensation plan to gain credibility, you must deal with both successes *and* failures. If, for example, an employee is simply not responding well to the new plan and is missing his or her targets for incentive payments, don't decide to pay that employee anyway. That would cause employees to discount the whole plan. Remember the fourfold need to be fair, to be clear, to be consistent, and to honor the plan. Just as it would be wrong not to pay what an employee earns, it would be wrong to pay what an employee does not earn.

### Don't Make It Only an Annual Ritual

Find reasons to discuss and trumpet your compensation plan (and its successes) at odd times in the year. If you celebrate the plan only in a paragraph in the annual report or a one-hour review at the management retreat once a year, you're underplaying the value of this exceptional retention tool and undermining its impact on retention.

Imbue your compensation plan with an identity: give it a name, maybe even a logo, and a "responsible officer." Send out bulletins from time to time on recent progress and awards. When making a bonus payment, don't just mail out a check— even with a thank-you letter from the CEO. Gather everyone in the department, stand on a table, and get a round of applause for the recipient. Work the plan!

### Remember the Personal Touch

No compensation plan can institutionalize what most people want from their employer—a recognition that they matter as individuals. Even the best compensation plan is no substitute for walking down to Juanita's desk, looking her in the eye, and saying, "Thank you."

## Manager's Checklist for Chapter 5

- ❑ Base pay, incentives, and benefits are *satisfiers*, not *motivators*.
- ❑ Bonuses, perks, and properly designed deferred compensation are true motivators.
- ❑ Adjusting compensation will only have a one-time effect, unless your compensation plan meets retention-specific goals and employees consider it to be fair, clear, consistent, and honored.
- ❑ Compare your compensation plan with best practices elsewhere, make any required adjustments, and then market the new compensation plan internally and externally.

# Employee Recognition: What Works, What Doesn't

*They pay you nickels and dimes, but this is what makes it worth it (referring to the presidential yacht, Sequoia).*
—Richard Nixon

*The last reward is the one remembered.*
—Anonymous

Designed and implemented correctly, recognition programs can play an important role in retaining top employees. Handled badly, they can be embarrassing irrelevancies, disdained by the employees, and rapidly fall into disuse. In this chapter we'll see how to ensure that your recognition program helps you retain top performers.

## Targeting Your Recognition Program to Top Employees

The first goal of your recognition program is to target the right people—in this case, top employees.

Of course, recognition programs don't *have* to be restricted to top employees (or even include them at all), but that's the

> **Employee recognition program** A program that recognizes outstanding achievements by employees with money and/or other assets. Recognition programs can combine structured, planned *awards* (such as an "employee of the month" award) with unplanned, spontaneous *rewards* (such as a reward for taking first place in a national professional examination) and/or *contests* (such as a quarterly sales contest or a safety improvement contest).

focus of this book so that's what we'll emphasize here. Later in this chapter, you'll learn how to combine recognition programs for top performers with recognition programs targeted at other employees.

### Know Who They Are

As a first step to targeting your recognition program, list the employees that you're likely to include. If you need any help in identifying your top performers, review the work you did in the first part of Chapter 3, Envisioning Your Employee Retention Strategy.

The next question is "Who should be included in the recognition program?"

If you don't have many top performers or if your organization has sufficient resources, the answer may well be "All of them." If, however, you're managing a lot of top performers or your resources are limited, you may wish to undertake a risk analysis to identify those top performers who are most likely to pose a retention risk in the near future and then to aim your recognition program at them.

> **Recognition Program "Mix"**
> Employee recognition programs can comprise any number of elements, restricted only by your imagination. The aim of this chapter is not to provide you with a list of reward ideas, but rather to ensure that, whichever rewards you use, you implement them in a way that will help you keep your top employees.
>
> For ideas about rewards, check out *1001 Ways to Reward Your Employees* by Bob Nelson (Workman Publishing, 1994). Nelson is the "rewards guru" and his book, newsletter, and excellent Web site (www.nelson-motivation.com) will provide you with more ideas than you thought possible!

**Risk Analysis**
A risk analysis would involve assessing each top employee (on a scale of 1 to 5, for example) on criteria such as their current and recent performance, skills, and ease of replacement. The result would be a ranking of employees in the order in which you should include them in a recognition program *at this time.*

Once you've identified the top employees to include in your recognition program, you need to consider the design. There are three options:

• Separate
• Tiered
• Modular

**Separate Program**

Should your recognition program be for top performers only, separate from other employees? In my experience, such an approach has substantial drawbacks, not least on the morale of those employees not involved in the recognition program. A separate, elite recognition program (for top performers only) *can* exist harmoniously under two conditions:

• There are clear outputs to be recognized that only top performers are likely to achieve.
• All other employees are receiving total compensation packages that are above the industry and job average.

If you're not meeting both of these conditions, consider a *tiered* program or a *modular* program.

**Tiered Program**

In most circumstances, recognition programs for top employees will run together with or as part of wider employee recognition programs. The most common way to do this is to have a "tiered" recognition program, where there are escalating rewards depending on the seniority of the employee and/or the level of achievement.

This approach works in most cases. But if a desired result of the recognition program for one particular group is very precise (such as the retention of top employees), designing a tiered program can be somewhat restricting, as the recognition program goals need to be expanded to be attractive to *all* employees (not just top employees and not just employees we wish to retain).

### Modular Program

As we've seen, a tiered approach to recognition can dilute the retention goals for top performers. In many circumstances, they can also alienate employees who feel they can't really compete with the top performers.

Far better is a *modular approach,* which allows for the design of separate recognition programs for different groups, under one overarching umbrella, such as beating sales targets or completing that tricky computer installation.

## Orienting Your Recognition Program Around Retention

You've achieved the first goal for the recognition program—targeting top performers. The second goal is to make sure it is retention-oriented.

Employee recognition programs suffer from the "mom and apple pie" syndrome: they are seen as all-round "good things to do" and rarely are viewed as having specific, measurable goals. "We're good employers," so the thinking goes, "so we provide employee recognition programs." However, if you want to retain your best employees, it's important that your recognition programs have a traceable, direct impact on your retention goal.

**Recognition Isn't Compensation**

In some cases, recognition programs are considered a low- or no-cost alternative to monetary compensation—usually by employers who aren't paying a fair wage. If your compensation packages aren't competitive, a recognition program won't rectify the situation. As we discussed at length in Chapter 5, you *must* get your compensation packages to market level before introducing other elements of the retention toolkit, including recognition packages—particularly to retain top employees.

### Addressing Multiple Goals, but with a Retention Focus

That is not to say that recognition programs cannot have multiple goals. Indeed, most do—whether to achieve product quality targets, beat sales targets, or improve workplace safety (for example), most recognition programs are designed on one or more operational goals as "hooks." In general, those goals are enough: meet these operational goals and we'll recognize your achievement.

To retain exceptional employees, however, designing recognition programs involves adding another layer.

### Outputs vs. Behaviors

The way to do this is to distinguish between *outputs* and *behaviors*:

- *Outputs* are the operational goals that underpin the recognition program, like achieving product quality targets, beating sales targets, or improving workplace safety.
- *Behaviors* are the ways in which employees meet or exceed those goals.

Identifying retention-related behaviors allows you to design a retention-focused recognition program.

### Awards vs. Rewards

Before we consider how to identify retention-related behaviors (and how to include them in a recognition program), we need a word about outputs and behaviors and how you can best recognize them in your programs.

By and large, it's best to recognize *outputs* (when achieved) through *awards* and *behaviors* through *rewards*.

Awards are perennial and they go to whoever gets closest to the goal. There's usually a plaque, shield, scroll, or other way of indicating that this *is* an award and will be bestowed again in the future. The Nobel Prizes and Olympic gold medals are good examples of awards.

Rewards are not necessarily given at all; if they're given, it's to recognize a behavior that deserves a reward, not just because someone came closest to what was desired.

Awards are given out automatically; rewards are not. Awards are planned; rewards are spontaneous.

## Designing Recognition Programs to Enhance Behaviors

So, to be effective, recognition programs targeted at retaining your best employees should focus on rewarding behaviors that are related to retention. Here are various ways of achieving the same thing:

- Design the recognition program so that, rather than saying to the employee, "Thanks" (for making sales, hitting product quality, maintaining workplace safety), it says, "I like the *way* you did that. Do it more."
- Focus on the *people* in the recognition program and less on the *outputs*.
- Reward the *how*, not the *what*.

OK, now what "retention-related behaviors" do we wish to encourage?

### Negotiable and Nonnegotiable Behaviors

The first distinction to be made is between *negotiable* behaviors and *nonnegotiable* behaviors.

Nonnegotiable behaviors are those actions that are expected of any employee, irrespective of "retention status"; it's the conduct you or your organization expect from all employees on all occasions. Although these will vary from organization to organization, characteristics such as behaving ethically, professionally, and with care and consideration for others are generally nonnegotiable behaviors.

Retention-related behaviors—behaviors that indicate and strengthen a commitment to the organization—are generally *negotiable* behaviors; they're attitudes and approaches that an employee may choose to exhibit at his or her discretion.

### Rewarding Behaviors and Encouraging Behaviors

With entry-level new hires, unskilled in the way of business, there may be a need to reward the development of positive nonnegotiable behaviors, through recognition programs and other tools such as mentoring, coaching, and positive feedback.

To make this learning process effective, it's important to continue to encourage those behaviors over time, not just during the orientation process. Positive behaviors are like muscles: they can become flabby with misuse. Don't run your recognition program once or twice, then remove all forms of support when you see the positive behaviors emerge. Continue to encourage retention-related behaviors regularly.

Employee recognition programs should be used to develop positive *negotiable* behaviors. Except for entry-level new hires (see above sidebar), if you have to use a recognition program to encourage *nonnegotiable* behaviors, there's something wrong with your hiring process!

### Examples of Retention-Related Behaviors

Here are some examples of behaviors that are indicators of positive retention attitudes in your top employees. Take time to add to the list and to consider ways in which you can reward these behaviors through your recognition program:

- Assimilating with the organization (e.g., learning acronyms, joining social groups, volunteering to arrange social events)
- Taking a long-term view (e.g., building relationships with clients and customers, planning and scheduling medium and long-term goals)
- Building team relationships (e.g., sharing bonuses or otherwise rewarding team members, cross-training other team members)
- Strengthening corporate culture (e.g., exhibiting core values, informally mentoring or coaching others).

## Designing Specific Recognition Goals

Whatever the constituent elements of your recognition program—rewards, awards, contests, or whatever else you decide to include—to be successful it's important to design each element in a way that's specific, attainable, fair, and appropriate.

### The Importance of Specificity

It's important that each recognition element be as *specific* as possible. In order to avoid confusion and, at worst, demotivating effects, make sure that all employees understand all of the important details of your recognition program—eligibility, quantities, quality, and the appraisal process.

> ### Testing Specificity
> TRICKS OF THE TRADE
>
> One of the simplest ways to know if the details of your recognition activity are specific enough is to test them in advance. Hand the terms and conditions of your program component to someone completely removed from the environment in which it will be used (friends and significant others come in handy at this point!) and ask what questions they have. Use their responses to develop the terms and conditions until all the obvious questions are answered.

First, it should be obvious to all employees whether or not they're entitled to take part in any element of a recognition program, particularly if you're using the modular approach.

Second, make sure there's no doubt about any quantifiable aspects of the recognition program. Whether it's a sales target, a safety goal, the number of days of free vacation you're giving away, or the deadline for a competition to end, anything that's quantifiable should be clear and unambiguous at the *outset*.

Otherwise, you risk reducing the impact of the program (it's hard to get excited about a reward for hitting a target if either the target or the reward is ill-defined) and losing credibility (there's always a lingering doubt that the numbers may be "massaged" at the end to achieve a preferred result).

### George Sets the Terms

George wants the new R&D scientists on his team to settle into cohesive operating teams, as he's observed this to be good for retention. He decides to make an award to the team that comes up with the greatest number of possible uses for a by-product of a manufacturing process.

He specifies the terms carefully:

• The contest closes at 5 p.m. on February 28.

• Each team must have met as a group on at least three occasions for at least 45 minutes each time.

• There will be one award, to the team with the most suggestions—a free meal at a local gourmet restaurant for all team members and one guest each, with no limit on the food element and a $10 per person limit on drinks.

Third, be specific about the *quality* of what you're offering. Particularly in dealing with top performers—who usually have high standards—it hurts the credibility of a recognition program if the quality of prizes and awards are hyped. Either don't scrimp on the quality of the awards or be ruthlessly honest about them.

### Keeping It Real...

I know one organization that had a very competitive monthly contest for a completely nondescript football shirt that was handed from winner to winner, rather like the yellow jersey in the Tour de France. No one complained about the quality of the shirt because there were no expectations: everyone knew it was merely symbolic and somewhat of a much-loved joke. On the other hand, a hyped "free vacation" that turns out to be three nights in a grubby motel in the back of beyond will only have a *negative* effect on retaining top employees.

Finally, make sure to specify the workings of the appraisal part of the recognition process—who decides who gets what? Treat your employees with respect and honesty—or you deserve the cynicism that's likely to result. If, for example, the "Employee of the Month" award is decided entirely on your whim on the last day of the month, say so! (Most employees will be able to figure out your judgment criteria after a few months, anyway, so why keep up the pretense that it's otherwise?)

## Ensuring That Your Targets Are Attainable

After nailing the specific, measurable elements of your recognition program, your next step is to ensure that any *targets* in your program are attainable. If your employees can't attain the targets you set, the program won't motivate your top performers and won't encourage retention.

Start by using past performance as a guide, if possible. Set the recognition program targets within the top 5%-15% of already achieved past results. There's little to gain in setting targets at a level previously unattained, unless you have good reason to believe those higher targets will be met.

Once you've set initial targets for your recognition program, make sure you take the time to solicit feedback from your employees, before you proceed. After all, since the goals are for the employees, not you, their views on whether or not the goals are attainable are more important than yours.

In some organizations, recognition programs are handed down to employees rather like the stone tablets from Mount Sinai—in a flurry of smoke and mirrors, with terms, conditions, goals, and rewards all neatly decided and carved in stone by management.

This approach only has the effect of imbuing the recognition program with a sense of paternalism. Why not start the

---

### Recognition vs. Performance Incentives

**Smart Managing**

Don't forget that recognition programs are not performance incentive programs. If you want to lift performance levels, design a performance incentive program to include stretch goals (goals set higher than past performance levels), as discussed in Chapter 5.

Stretch goals do not make good recognition program targets because if they're not met, there's usually a sense of failure and disappointment—the exact opposite of what you're trying to engender with a recognition program: a sense of success and achievement.

**Be Sure You Have What It Takes**

Do you have the resources to pay awards, make vacation arrangements, give frequent flier miles, or whatever else you're promising as recognition? It is, unfortunately, far from uncommon for organizations not to deliver on promises made in recognition programs. The impact on retention is easy to predict.

recognition process right, by recognizing that your best performers probably have a lot to contribute to the design and implementation of an effective recognition process?

## Setting Fair Outcomes

After ensuring that your recognition program is *specific* and *attainable*, the next "pre-launch check" is this: Is it fair? If not, your recognition program will only build resentment and cynicism.

**Anticipating the Implications of Implementation**

Especially when dealing with top performers, where rewards can be substantial, you must anticipate the implications of implementing a recognition program. As part of its recognition program, one company I know very well (I was the co-founder) paid for selected top employees to attend Harvard Business School for a six-week course each summer for three years. Unfortunately, no one thought through the operational implications of losing a key executive for six weeks. The company had to drop the scheme.

First, is the program fair to the employees for whom it's designed? There are three main ways in which an employee recognition program can be unfair to the employees involved:

• The program fosters negative competition among employees. No employee should have to stand on the heads of others to achieve recognition. Recognition programs that foster negative competition are bad for retention.

• The program requires employees to neglect their regular responsibilities. Recognition programs should not be used as a back door to persuading employees to take on additional duties for little or no

---

**Be Careful with Contests**

Many recognition programs include contests. This seems appropriate, especially with employees you want to retain who have a developed sense of competition. Bear in mind, however, that contests often breach the first of the three caveats listed above by setting employees against one another. Also, contests produce winners and losers—an outcome inappropriate in a recognition program. Recognition programs should produce *only* winners, not losers. If employees are underperforming, address the problem through the performance management process, not the employee recognition program.

---

actual pay. Some "recognition programs" are little more than ham-handed attempts to get employees to do more for less.

- The program makes an inordinate demand on the employees' personal time and/or resources. You should recognize achievements attainable within normal working schedules. It's often amazed me that organizations set up "work-life balance" programs for their employees while designing recognition programs that reward only those employees who work substantially outside normal working hours.

If your top employees work mostly in teams, consider making the recognition process team-oriented. Setting individual recognition goals is fine, but not if it tears at team structure. Remember: teamwork isn't always a top performer's strong point and, as we've seen earlier in this chapter, engendering quality teamwork should be one of the goals of your top employee recognition program. If that means making the entire program team-oriented, like George and his R&D team (see sidebar on page 108), that's fine.

You want your recognition program to positively impact the retention of your top employees—but not at the cost of negatively impacting the retention of other employees.

Make sure that the rewards and awards in your module for your best performers aren't unfairly "rich" in comparison with those offered to other employees. Otherwise, you'll end up with

> **Use the Golden Ratio**
> A good general rule is to keep the value of rewards and awards in the same ratio as total compensation. Thus, employee "A," who earns a total of $50,000 per annum and is eligible for a recognition award worth $2,000, is likely to view as reasonably equitable that employee "B," who earns a total of $100,000 per annum, is eligible for an award worth $4,000. However, if employee "B" were to be eligible for a recognition award of $10,000, employee "A" might sense that the arrangement is unfair.
>
> *Note:* This is simple enough for monetary awards, but you might need to convert non-monetary awards to a dollar value to make the same estimate.

disgruntled employees—many of whom will be providing essential support for your top performers and will be acutely aware of any perceived inequities.

Finally, if you're considering implementing a recognition program for your top people, make sure this program is fair to the organization as a whole. There are three ways in which a divisional or departmental recognition program can be detrimental to the organization:

- The program takes key people out of the loop. Make sure your recognition program does not divert key people from other organizational responsibilities. (See the sidebar on page 110, "Anticipating the Implications of Implementation," for an example.)

> **Watch Fairness to the Customers**
> Be attentive to the impact of your recognition program on your clients and customers, particularly if it includes sales contests. Make sure that contests don't place your top employees in a position where, in order to win, they're stuffing the sales channel or otherwise treating customers unfairly.

- The program sets unfair expectations. Run the goals and any rewards and awards past your colleagues to ensure you're not setting any unreasonable expectations for other employees in the organization.

- The program distorts established standards or processes. Watch that goals or targets that you choose to reward aren't standard performance goals for other employees in the organization.

## Making Recognition Programs Appropriate

It's important that recognition programs be not only specific, attainable, and fair, but also *appropriate*. This means ensuring that rewards and awards are relevant in type and level to top performers.

### Monetary Rewards

The most important thing to bear in mind about monetary rewards is that they should not be so large that they're a material element of compensation. If the monetary rewards available to an employee through a recognition program amount to more than around 15% of total monetary compensation, employees will begin to view them as an element of compensation, like a discretionary bonus, rather than as recognition.

> **Put the Money into Bonuses**
>
> If you do want to make large amounts of money available to your employees, put it into a bonus system, as discussed in Chapter 5. Don't forget: recognition programs are to recognize achievements that are out of the ordinary and bonus programs are to incite greater production. Don't confuse the two.

### Non-Monetary Rewards

Similar considerations of materiality apply to non-monetary rewards, like giveaways, vacations, or paid time off. Convert the reward to its monetary value (if it has one) and do the same math. If the value is greater than around 15% of total compensation, it's too high.

Here are some other considerations to bear in mind in making your non-monetary rewards relevant:

- **Expectations.** Top employees are less likely to be excit-

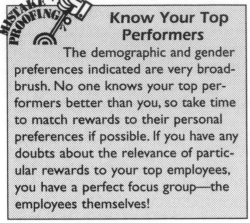

### Know Your Top Performers

The demographic and gender preferences indicated are very broad-brush. No one knows your top performers better than you, so take time to match rewards to their personal preferences if possible. If you have any doubts about the relevance of particular rewards to your top employees, you have a perfect focus group—the employees themselves!

ed by pens, T-shirts, and even quality luggage sets and vacations than by rewards that reflect their position. Try building your program to include rewards that:

– Provide access to senior management (e.g., inclusion in a senior management retreat).

– Reflect and emphasize autonomy (e.g., paid time off and telecommuting resources).

– Support cutting-edge development (e.g., technology— PDAs, instant messaging systems).

- **Demographic preferences.** Again, as a general indicator only (see the sidebar, "Know Your Top Performers"), employees under 35 are often more likely to select "lifestyle" rewards such as holidays and sporting equipment, while employees over 35 more often appreciate monetary  rewards or flexible work schedules.

### Yankees Tickets Don't Travel

A large insurance organization based in New York had a rewards program for its top sales performers, which included tickets for the New York Yankees. Unfortunately, 35% of the eligible employees were based in offices elsewhere than in New York. Those employees didn't hold the program in high esteem, because if they won they could benefit from the prize only at major expense to themselves.

- **Gender preferences.** Surveys regularly indicate that women prefer rewards that help them develop work-life balance (like paid time off and telecommuting resources), while men are more likely to prefer monetary rewards and "gizmos."

- **Impact of location.** If you manage employees who are dispersed in various locations, be careful not to design your rewards program with a "home office" bias.

## Communicating Your Recognition Program

The "secretsauce" in an effective recognition program for top employees is in the communication process. So many good employee suggestion programs, "employee of the month" programs, and sales target contests fall into disuse simply because the programs aren't communicated well enough. We'll close this chapter with some suggestions to help you communicate *your* program successfully.

**Planning.** Use the planning stage to build expectations and excitement. Don't design your recognition program behind closed doors, then unveil it. Take time to consult and communicate with your top employees right from the start.

> ### Form a Steering Committee
> Consider forming a steering committee of top employees to help you design and implement your recognition program. They'll bring good ideas and on-the-ground reactions—and also build word-of-mouth "buzz" about the program.
>
> *Tricks of the Trade*

**Selection of recognition program elements.** Consult fully with employees about the individual elements in your program. Seek their advice on whether to include "employee of the month" awards, "suggestion of the year" awards, safety awards, sales awards, etc. Again, their input will be invaluable in assessing the validity of the program *and* they'll help build expectations.

**Implementation.** Most organizations communicate only when they launch their recognition programs. But a single

> ### E-mail Is Great!
> Use e-mail to send out regular reminders of how the recognition program works. Don't be afraid to send exactly the same e-mail more than once—on launch day, a month later, three months after that, and then quarterly thereafter. You don't need to come up with something new every time; just reiterate the basics.
>
> *Smart Managing*

launch announcement is not very effective. Communicate the basics of your recognition program five to seven times in the first three months. Promote the launch and then reinforce the message using newsletters, employee notice boards, your corporate intranet, brown-bag lunches and any other means.

**Award time.** Make the most of award presentations. Get everyone to attend, whether they've won or not. Build up the event a little, including some ritual and fun. If possible, get a member of senior management to present the awards and (bearing in mind that you're dealing with high performing employees) provide the winners with as much exposure as possible.

## Manager's Checklist for Chapter 6

❑ Recognition programs can be a major help in retaining top employees—if designed to be retention-oriented.

❑ Ensure that your program rewards retention-related behaviors as well as outputs.

❑ Your recognition program must be specific, attainable, fair and appropriate.

❑ Effective communication is essential to the success of your recognition program.

# Recruiting for Retention

*I'm not hiring for where I am; I'm hiring for where I'll be.*
—Fred Bramante Jr.,
CEO, Daddy's Junky Music, Inc

*We don't start out with the assumption that our company is for everybody.*
—William G. McGowan
Former chairman and founder,
MCI Communications Corp.

So far, we've envisioned what our retention strategy will *achieve*, we've set realistic *goals* for our retention activities, and we've identified the *major elements* of our retention strategy. Now it's time to start *implementing* our strategy.

Where will you start implementing your retention strategy? Well, the best place to start is the point at which you first interact with potential employees—the recruiting process.

Do you remember the five-phase golf swing analogy outlined in Chapter 2?

---

### Don't Wait Too Long

Many managers wait too long before implementing their employee retention strategy. It's natural to want to make sure everything is "planned right" before beginning implementation, but it's a mistake. Implementation is not the end of the planning process; it's part of it.

It's important to start implementing your retention strategy as soon as possible, because it's only then that you can begin to adjust it according to the realities of your own organizational culture.

Don't succumb to "paralysis by analysis." Get started now!

---

1. Picturing the Shot: Envisioning Your Retention Strategy
2. Club Selection: Deciding Which Retention Tools to Use
3. Backswing: Recruiting for Retention
4. Point of Impact: Making the Difference with Orientation
5. Follow-Through: Maintaining Retention Through the Employment Life Cycle

We've finished the first two phases (Picturing the Shot and Club Selection). Now, let's start phase three—Backswing!

## What Is Recruiting for Retention?

At some point, all organizations recruit employees. Only some organizations (surprisingly, very few) *recruit for retention*.

The difference? Figure 7-1 summarizes the main dis-

---

### Learn from Your Competitors

**Smart Managing**   Can you or your fellow managers identify an organization in your industry that seems to be great at retaining good employees? If so, spend an hour pretending you're thinking about working for that organization. Look at their Web site, their job ads, their recruitment materials. If they have a job hotline, call it and ask for more details on a specific position. If you can, visit a hiring fair or other function where you can see their recruiting team at work.

Don't worry about analyzing the results of your investigation; what's important is to experience their recruiting process. Take time to note down the three features of their recruiting activities that most impressed you as a prospective employee.

---

| | Generic Recruitment | Recruiting for Retention |
|---|---|---|
| Employment Contract | Hires to the old employment contract. | Hires to the new employment contract. |
| Hiring Model | Concentrates mostly on the classic hiring model. | Uses all hiring models. |
| Employee Profile | Based on function and skills. | Based on function, skills, and "fit." |
| Hiring Methods | Emphasizes speed and "place-filling." Event-related. | Emphasizes alignment between employee and employer. Process-based. |

Figure 7-1. The main differences between generic recruiting and recruiting for retention

tinctions between *generic recruiting* (what most organizations do) and *recruiting for retention* (what organizations with excellent retention do). Don't worry if some of these phrases seem unfamiliar to you. In the rest of this chapter, we'll discuss each of the main differences in turn.

## The Employment Contract

The first major difference between those organizations that merely recruit and those that recruit for retention is the implicit *employment contract* between the employee and the employer.

### The Old Employment Contract

Historically, the "employment contract" was essentially a statement of the status quo. The employer would in effect say to the

> **Key Term**
> **Employment contract**
> The *implicit, overall* relationship between the employer and the employee. Although the term "employment contract" is also used, of course, for the legal document that sometimes defines the terms of employment, what we're considering in this chapter is the relationship.

employee, "You come work for me, I'll pay you, and so long as you do a good job, you can stay."

This so-called "lifetime" employment contract—hire competent people, pay them, they stay with you—was ideally suited to the industrial age, when labor was (relatively) cheap, the workforce was static, and economic cycles were longer and more predictable.

However, over the last 15 years, the "lifetime" employment contract has been rendered less and less relevant by demographic and economic shifts, primarily these five:

1. Increased employee *mobility*. It's easier (and cheaper) for an employee to relocate to a new job than 15 years ago.
2. *Economic constraints*. The boom-and-bust economic cycle has made it impossible for organizations to credibly offer "lifetime" employment.
3. The need for frequent *upskilling*. Reduced product cycle times and increased consumer demand has made it less likely that an employee's *skills set* will remain relevant and sufficient over time, thus reducing the employee's employability over the long term.
4. The move to a *knowledge-based economy*. In the past, training (and therefore job security) was largely controlled by the employer. The rise of lifelong learning and the availability of distance learning have freed the employee to pursue his or her own career development. As a result, people are able to move from job to job with greater ease.
5. The rise of the *portfolio career*. As a result of demographic and economic shifts 1, 3, and 4, employees today are much less likely to be looking for a "job for life" in any one organization (the premise of the "lifetime" employment contract). Instead, employees are building career portfolios con-

**Skills set** The knowledge, experience, and qualifications of an employee relevant to his or her job. Hundreds of years ago, the skills set of a carpenter or a mason, for example, might not change much, if at all, over their lifetime. Today, employees must improve and develop their skills set constantly to remain employable.

sisting of a series of jobs, each lasting from two to 10 years.

### The New Employment Contract

In response to the pressures detailed above, the employment contract has changed radically over the last few years. Now, instead of making the unrealistic assumption of "employment for life," organizations that are *recruiting for retention* hire to a *new* employment contract that recognizes these new realities in the workplace. In the new employment contract, a person says to an employer, "I will come work for you, so long as you make me more employable and pay me a fair salary. I will remain with you so long as I am being challenged and developed as an individual."

Notice the important, changed elements in the new employment contract:

1. It is not assumed that employment is for life. There is an explicit acceptance that, in time, the employee will move on.
2. The continuance of the employment is predicated on the development of the employee, not the employer's needs.
3. To the employee, compensation is often secondary in importance to personal and skills set development.

> **Lifelong learning** The regular development and extension of the employee's skills set, often (though not always) at the employee's cost and in the employee's own time. We will return to this phrase often, since providing lifelong learning opportunities is a major element in effective employee retention.

> ### Who's Making the Decision?
> **Smart Managing**
>
> Notice the change in voice between the two employment contracts. The *old* employment contract is in the *employer's voice*, reflecting the balance of power in the old way of hiring. The *new* employment contract is in the *employee's voice*, reflecting a shift in that balance of power.
>
> Smart managers realize that nowadays, more often than not, the employee chooses the employer, not the other way around.

### The Implications for Recruiting for Retention

What are the implications of this shift in employment contracts? Well, for organizations wishing to *recruit for retention*, here are the main learning points:

- Understand that potential employees are making a choice about *you* as an employer, not the other way around. **Question:** If this concept is new to you, what changes are needed in your hiring methods, your employment literature, and your interview techniques to reflect this new reality?
- Accept the fact that the need for lifelong learning and personal development means that most employees will leave your organization in due course to pursue other options. **Question:** What have you been assuming is a *normal, reasonable* period of time an employee should stay with you? Many managers assume unrealistically—five years, 10 years, or more. This is based on *old* employment contract thinking. A much more realistic assumption is that most employees will stay around two to three years and that four or five years is excellent retention.
- Realize that compensation is only *one reason* why employees stay, and that it's often secondary to their personal and career development. **Question:** Review your employment literature, your Web site, and other resources you make available to prospective employees. Note the balance between the information you provide on compensation and the information you provide on personal and career development. Is the balance reasonable in light of the *new* employment contract? Or is there too much emphasis on compensation-related aspects and not enough on personal and career development?

Now that we've considered the importance of using the *new employment contract* as a basis for hiring, let's move on to the *second* major difference between those organizations that recruit for retention and those that merely recruit.

## The New Hiring Model(s)

As we saw in Figure 7-1, the second main difference between those organizations that are merely recruiting and those that are recruiting for retention is that recruiting for retention involves understanding (and using) the fact that there's more than one *hiring model.*

**Change Your Point of View**

If your mindset is determined by the *old* employment contract thinking, you view every good employee who leaves as a failure, an indication of a retention problem. If you adopt the realities of the new employment contract, you'll understand that *some* employee turnover is expected and healthy.

Under the *old* employment contract, there was in essence only one hiring model—that of the *core employee.* An organization would hire people and those employees would stay with that organization for so long as the status quo prevailed.

However, as we've noted (p. 120), in the last 15 years, demographic and economic factors have rendered the old employment contract less and less relevant. Fewer employees *want* to be "core," "lifetime" employees; in fact, many feel uncomfortable in such an environment. This discomfort—a lack of "fit" with the employer—is a major contributor to

**Core employee** An employee of the organization who works only for that organization, at its place of business, undertaking such tasks as directed by his or her employer. Core employment can be full- or part-time.

employee turnover. As we've seen in earlier chapters, *people stay where they feel at home* and employees typically won't feel at home (and will therefore eventually leave) if the basis on which they've been employed is inappropriate to their needs.

In response, organizations seeking to recruit for retention have developed *other hiring models,* reducing the centrality of the core employee concept and reflecting more accurately the needs of their prospective employees.

There are *five common hiring models* being used by organizations that recruit for retention. Each of them has different advantages for the employer seeking to maximize employee retention.

### Model 1: The Classic Model—Core Employees

We've already discussed the concept of the core employee: it's the standard hiring model. This model works best in circumstances such as the following:

- Senior management appointments, where you want and need the person's full time and attention
- Core activities, when the job is central to the purpose of your organization
- Proprietary activities, where there are trade secrets or intellectual copyrights that you wish to keep internal

Many organizations make the mistake of assuming that the core employee is the *only* hiring model available to them and try to shoehorn every job into this model, with the dysfunctional result detailed above. In fact, using other hiring models appropriately is a vital step in recruiting for retention.

### Model 2: Flexible Work

As we've seen, over the last 15 years the relevance of core employment status has been weakened by a combination of

---

**TRICKS OF THE TRADE**                **Polishing the Apple**

Consider making core employment with your company a cherished status. Using the core employment model *selectively* will add luster to this type of position.

Your hiring practices should reflect reality—that true core employees are becoming less and less common. Reverse the usual employment psychology: make non-core employment the *norm* (by using some of the other hiring models) and core employment a *goal* to be attained.

Consider changing the "default" hiring status in your company to one of the other hiring models. Make it clear to candidates that they need to persuade you to offer them core employee status.

economic and demographic changes in the workplace, particu
larly the following:

- The rise in employee mobility
- The availability of inexpensive communications and com-
  puter networking technologies
- The rise in working single parents
- Pressure on employers to minimize costs.

Responding to these pressures, employers aiming to recruit
for retention have developed several versions of core employee
status that don't require that employees work in a specific place
and/or at a specific time: *telecommuting, job sharing,* and the
*compressed workweek.*

**Telecommuting.** Telecommuting gives employees all the benefits of core employee status, but frees them to work at a place
or time of their own choosing. The telecommuting model works
best with these types of jobs:

- Non-team-based positions. Collaborative technologies
  such as videoconferencing cannot yet fully replace face-
  to-face interaction, although computer technology will
  eventually overcome this limitation.
- Administrative positions. Jobs involving intensive interaction with computer databases are ideal for telecommuting.
- Sales and marketing
  activities. Where it's
  possible (and per-
  haps desirable) for
  employees to set
  their own schedules
  for visiting cus-
  tomers, clients, or
  other company sites,
  telecommuting is
  ideal.

If you're going to use

**Forms Processing**
In the late '70s, many U.S.-
based insurance companies
started using the telecommuting
model for intensive off-site forms
processing. Many companies established large forms processing net-
works based in Southern Ireland, taking advantage of the difference in time
zones to allow access to their computer databases during the cheaper
(and less busy) night hours.

**Smart Managing**

**Ask Your Professional Advisor** Much of the concept of telecommuting was developed in professional firms, such as attorneys and accountants. They pioneered the concept of hot-desking, then found that telecommuting was a natural next step and an ideal hiring model for many of their employees. If you're thinking of using the telecommuting hiring model, speak to your professional advisors: they may be using that model already and be able to advise you.

telecommuting as a hiring model, it's imperative to establish clear reporting and administrative procedures so that your employees don't feel "cast adrift" from the organization. Telecommuters must be involved as much as possible in the day-to-day ebb and flow of corporate interaction.

**Job Sharing.** Developed particularly in response to the dramatic rise in the number of single parents in the workplace, job sharing allows two or more people to share a single job by working at different times and/or on separate days. Job-sharing employees may also be telecommuting. Job sharing works well for jobs where:

- *There's no strong need for continuity of individual interaction with customers or other third parties.* For example, job sharing will work well in a *call center*, where customers calling do not expect to deal with the same employee each time. It will work less well in *key account selling*, where each customer needs to deal with the same employee.
- *The degree of internal team interaction is low.* Where other employees are involved, keeping each of the job-sharing employees "up to speed" on developments can become frustrating. For example, buying advertising for an organization is ideal for job sharing, as it's a discrete task that can be completed alone. On the other hand, brainstorming over three or four sessions with the advertising team on a new campaign is less suitable for job sharing, because shifting from one employee to another between sessions disrupts the continuity.

- *The individual job tasks are linear, discrete, and short-term.* Where the job being shared involves tasks that are wide-ranging and long-term (for example, pharmaceutical R&D), it isn't practicable to "hand over" the job once a day or even every few days. Each employee will want to pursue his or her own train of thought and the nature of the tasks doesn't allow for easy summation and handover. On the other hand, a machine operator on a factory production line can hand over a job to a colleague with a minimum of interaction required.

> **Watch Cost Creep**
>
> Job sharing can be an excellent addition to your retention efforts, but if you decide to use it as a hiring model, watch the underlying *costs of employment.* Job sharing often results in duplication of costs for tools, computer equipment, training programs, and other resources that each employee needs for the job. Be strict in ensuring that any duplication of costs is necessary. Where practical, enforce sharing *resources* as well as sharing *jobs.*

**Compressed Workweek.** Many organizations now realize that some jobs that require a commitment of 40 hours a week can be done in different "rhythms," often more suited to their employees' commitments or preferences. Two compressed workweek schedules are common:

- Four 10-hour days
- Five nine-hour days, followed by four nine-hour days (i.e., a day off every two weeks)

Compressed workweeks best suit jobs that involve little interaction with colleagues (who may not be available when the "compressed" employee is clocking those late or early hours) and no direct interaction with customers or clients (who may not appreciate being contacted at times outside "normal work hours").

I predict that the compressed workweek will be the fastest growing form of flexible work over the next few years, for two reasons:

**Cut Commute Burnout**

**Smart Managing** Compressed workweeks can be great where employees face particularly brutal commutes. Where I live (just outside San Francisco), the Friday evening commute is especially severe and begins as early as 2:30 p.m. Many organizations here use a variant of the compressed workweek to help their employees escape that particular form of purgatory!

1. Many people are becoming accustomed to working longer: 10- and 12-hour days are now becoming much more common.
2. Coupled with this lengthening of the workday, there's an almost contradictory desire to attain a better work-life balance, to have more opportunity to enjoy leisure time.

Compressed workweeks allow reconciliation of these paradoxical pressures. Employees are then much more likely to "feel at home" and so more likely to stay in their jobs.

**Resources to Help with the Flexible Work Model.** The Internet has become useful for employers deploying and managing flexible workers. There are many great Web sites that provide excellent resources for using the flexible work model. Here are some of the most popular Internet resources at the time this book went to press:

- **www.executiveworks.com.** Internet-based software that provides comprehensive tools to allow employees (as well as contractors and vendors) to manage themselves, including collaboration tools for project management and reporting purposes.
- **www.workoptions.com.** A great site covering all aspects of flexible working, this is a particularly interesting resource as it's written from the *employee's* perspective.
- **www.knowledgepoint.com.** This division of professional mega-publisher CCH offers all the tools you need to produce policies and procedures to cover flexible work.

## Model 3: Free Agents

The next natural step from flexible work is to recognize that there are many individuals out there who are eminently qualified to undertake a job for you, but who do not want to work full-time for one company, as a core employee or even as a flexible worker.

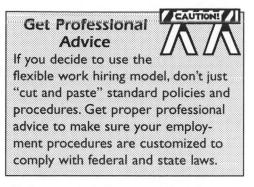

**Get Professional Advice**

If you decide to use the flexible work hiring model, don't just "cut and paste" standard policies and procedures. Get proper professional advice to make sure your employment procedures are customized to comply with federal and state laws.

The last three years have seen an enormous increase in the number of "free agents," as defined and described in Chapter 1—individuals who want the flexibility of self-employment.

As we noted in Chapter 1, the concept of free agency (made popular by Dan Pink, author of the definitive work on free agents: *Free Agent Nation: How America's New Independent Workers Are Transforming the Way We Live*) reached its peak during the dot-com boom of 1998-2000. Although the growth in the number of free agents has certainly slowed in recent years, the idea of using free agents as a hiring model is very much here to stay.

Using free agents as a hiring model is particularly appropriate in the following situations:

**Free Agents**

Who are free agents? Consultants, of course, but also welders, accountants, plastic extrusion plant operatives, and so on: there are free agents doing almost eveything. Counting "the self-employed, freelancers, 'e-lancers,' independent contractors, home-based businesspeople, solo practitioners, independent professionals, and operators of microbusinesses," according to Dan Pink, author of *Free Agent Nation*, there are at least 30 million free agents in the U.S. alone.

- *The job is discrete and measurable.* Free agents, not being direct employees on a salary, are often paid on results. This works best where the output of the job is quantifiable (for example, number of square feet of fence painted or length of time to complete an approved patent application).

- *The skills required are not* core *to the business.* Free agents are usually *project-oriented.* If the job requires skills that are core to your business (i.e., you have an ongoing need for them), then you'd be better off using the core employee hiring model.
- *The skills required are rare and/or expensive.* If a task requires a specific skills set that your core employees are unlikely to possess (for example, a sheet metal manufacturer wishing to install a Web site database), then a free agent hiring model may be best.

## Model 4: Outsourcing

So far, we've examined how you can improve retention by changing the hiring model to accommodate more than just the core employee, to make your environment more suited to your employees, so they feel more at home and are thus more likely to stay with you longer.

The next logical step is to ask, "Why hire employees to do this job?"

Many organizations have concluded at some time that whole parts of their business operations consist of activities in which they shouldn't really be engaged at all. They've decided that, instead of trying to engage in these activities, they should either close them down or hand them over to other organizations and simply purchase the outputs.

Why would any organization do this? Well, there are a couple of reasons:

- *Vertical integration gone awry.* Sometimes

**Compaq Computers**
In July 2001, Compaq announced that it would no longer manufacture chips for its computers. Although Compaq had its own chip manufacturing plants (as a result of its 1998 acquisition of Digital Equipment Corporation), management decided that it could not compete effectively with dedicated chip manufacturers such as Intel and Advanced Micro Devices.

an organization will seek to protect itself from rises in the prices of materials it uses by producing the materials itself (vertical integration). Then, over time, it becomes clear that the organization simply cannot compete with the benefits of scale that the larger manufacturers enjoy and is in effect paying *more* for its materials than if it purchased them on the open market.

- *Overestimating core skills.* An organization experiencing a prolonged period of success may assume that it can work its "magic" on other products or services and acquires businesses in allegedly "related" industries. Then the new businesses prove to be a bad match with the organization's core skills.

Do you have a department, a division, or even just a team of people in this situation?

- The activity is not core to your business.
- Other organizations are producing the same product or service cheaper, faster, or both.
- It has difficulties with employee retention.

**The Virgin Group**

Following the great success of Virgin Airlines, Richard Branson (CEO of The Virgin Group) concluded that Virgin obviously had skills in the transportation industry in general—not just the airline business. As a result, Virgin spent many years and many millions of pounds grappling with the UK train network—which turned out to be a very different business altogether and much less responsive to the Virgin "magic."

If so, then trying solely to resolve the retention issues may prove unfruitful and you may need to consider recommending that your organization sell the unit and outsource the function.

## Model 5: Pushing the Work Down to Your Customers

This is a final way to change your hiring model to reduce retention problems. Consider the interface between you and your customer. Do you have retention difficulties at that point? Do you find it difficult to train and keep good employees in customer service, installation, and support? If so, one solution is to "outsource" the activity *directly to the customer.*

Many organizations have concluded that it's just not possible for them to find, train, motivate, and retain employees to do a good job on some of the tasks involved in customer interaction. So, they've "outsourced" the job directly to the customer. Examples surround us: drive-up ATMs, self-assembly furniture, "bag-your-own" groceries, downloadable books on the Web (which the customers print using *their* printer and *their* paper and ink).

This hiring model works best with:

- *Low-value transactions.* If you're in the automotive business, some customers may be happy to install their own mufflers, but if you're selling Bentleys, customers don't want to put the wheels on themselves.
- *Low-tech, uncomplicated activities.* If you sell furniture, your customers may accept (maybe even enjoy) a degree of self-assembly, but when the assembly manual gets to 15 pages and there are 278 screws, bolts, and washers involved, you'll lose business, except from the most die-hard DIY fans.
- *Non-critical activities.* A canny stock investor might undertake some investment research, maybe even conduct trades online, but when it comes to estate planning, the stakes are typically too high for most investors to do this themselves.

## Manager's Checklist for Chapter 7

❏ Review your recruiting activities. To which employment contract are you hiring—the *old* or the *new*?

❏ If you're still hiring to the *old* contract, list the changes you need to make to the employment literature and other materials you make available to prospective employees, your Web site, your job specifications, and your interviewing techniques to shift to the *new* employment contract.

> ### Think Creatively
>
> **Tricks of the Trade**
>
> Don't underestimate the power of "allowing" customers to do certain things for themselves that you're struggling to do right— or the effect on employee morale and retention.
>
> For many years, I co-owned and managed the Pizza Hut franchise in Ireland. An area of customer service that we handled badly was putting leftovers into "doggie bags" for the customers to take home. It was a messy, inconvenient, labor-intensive process that interrupted the flow of the waiters' and busboys' other tasks. As a result, we were slow and unresponsive at a time when customers just wanted to leave the restaurant. We didn't do this task well: we knew it and the customers knew it too. It seriously affected morale on busy shifts.
>
> Eventually, we began providing the customers with an area where they could bag their leftovers themselves. We simply set out everything they needed and periodically cleaned the area. It was a roaring success: the customers did the bagging and our employees were free to do their other tasks.

❑ Review your hiring models. Are you only using the core employee model?

❑ List the other hiring models that you could use in your organization. Match each hiring model you will use with a list of *specific jobs or positions* for which each would be appropriate.

❑ How flexible are your hiring processes, particularly with regard to flexible work and free agents? Do you have contracts and processes to encourage hiring free agents? Are you frequenting the hiring markets that free agents use (particularly the Internet)?

❑ Which activities are you currently undertaking that you should outsource to third parties?

❑ What activities can you outsource to your customers? Could you assign a task force to look at which aspects of your activities can be pushed down to customers?

# Making the Difference with Orientation

*Going to work for a large company is like getting on a train. Are you going sixty miles an hour or is the train going sixty miles an hour and you're just sitting still?*
—J. Paul Getty (1892-1976)

In the last two chapters, we examined what constitutes an effective "backswing"—recruitment activities that have a lasting impact on employee retention. In this chapter we discuss the point where "the club head meets the ball"—when the new employee arrives on board. We'll look at the vital role that effective orientation plays in retaining top employees. In particular we'll hit the following points:

- There's a vital link between orientation and retention.
- There's no such thing as "no orientation."
- Your orientation program should meet two short-term and three medium-term retention goals.

## The Link Between Retention and Orientation

As we saw in Chapter 2, if the face of the golf club is out of alignment when the club hits the ball, the ball will end up far away from our target. So it is with employee retention. You've set the retention goals you wish to achieve (pictured the shot, Chapter 3), selected the right retention tools (made the club selection, Chapters 4, 5, and 6), and communicated effectively pre-hire (backswing, Chapters 7). Now you reach the point of impact, when the employee joins your organization. This is a crucial point.

In a new employee's first few days, the organization sets the direction in which the employee will travel. If the organization is out of alignment with its employees at this point, there can be no surprise if weeks, months, or years later it finds that it has missed its retention targets. The key to ensuring that employees start off in the right direction toward your retention goal is *effective orientation*.

Let's be frank about this—orientation is the Cinderella of training. Despite being the most-attended training process on the planet, orientation is considered "boring," "crashingly dull," "tedious," "time-consuming," "wasteful," and "difficult" ... to quote just some of the milder words I've heard used.

As a result, orientation is often done badly—if at all. Consequently, it gets a bad name and becomes either a mostly ignored "junior playpen" for trainers to test their wings or a sleep-inducing non-event—or, worst of all, both.

---

**Retention Rejuvenates Orientation**

Smart Managing

In the mid- to late 1990s, the issue of employee retention put the importance of an effective orientation program back on top of the agenda for many employers. Organizations that already had an effective orientation program had a competitive edge.

Don't let your orientation program be *only* an adjunct of your retention activities. There are sound operational reasons why an effective orientation program is essential for *all* organizations—whether they have difficulties with retention or not.

## Sorry, I Didn't Notice You Standing There

And yet, remember our initial premise regarding retention: "People stay where they feel at home."

How does this picture of orientation (dull, tedious, poorly done) square with the idea of employees feeling at home in the organization? What's the effect of negligible or no orientation on your new employees' sense of being at home?

Here's an important principle: the employer-employee relationship is just that—a *relationship*. And, as in every other relationship, *first impressions count*. In a social environment, we mostly make our minds up about someone within 30 seconds of meeting that person. Then, only very hard work on their part will convince us that our first impressions were wrong.

It's exactly the same in business: your employees make up their minds about whether they feel at home or not in the first three weeks with you. If those first impressions are poor, it takes very hard work to convince them that they were wrong.

---

**MISTAKE PROOFING**

### The Time Window Is Small

Previously, in the "status quo" employment relationship, most new employees intended to stay with their new employer indefinitely. That usually meant at least five years, often much longer. That gave employers plenty of time to correct early relational mistakes—like a poor orientation program or none at all.

Now, however, employees feel much less pressure to hang around. They need to stay only 18 months or so (considerably less in some industries and particularly in the service sector) to avoid an unseemly blot on their résumés. If you fail to make your employees feel at home from the get-go, you don't have long to try to compensate.

It's a bit like the difference between the movies and TV. Movie producers can take time positioning a story, setting up characters, and building a plot. The moviegoers have paid their money to spend two hours in the darkened theater with no other distractions. TV is different. Fail to get the viewers' attention in the first 30 seconds and your program is toast. Out comes the remote and they're gone.

These days, hiring and keeping top employees is much more like making a TV program than a movie—you have to get their interest from the start!

> ### Your Computer Is in the Mail
> I once worked with a software design company that took eight weeks on average to provide each new programmer hired with the desk, chair, telephone, computer, software, e-mail access, and appropriate passwords that the employees needed *as a minimum* to do their job effectively.
>
> That's a long time to leave a new employee unproductive, even ignoring the considerable implications for the new employee's motivation, integration, and retention.

## There's No Such Thing as "No Orientation"

When I talk with managers about what they do to retain their top employees, they're often surprised when I ask about their orientation program. They often tell me, "Oh, we don't have an orientation program at that level—orientation is only for our entry-level employees (or shop floor employees, or production staff, or…)."

Here's a surprise: there's *no such thing* as having no orientation.

When you take on new employees and then you do nothing—from the start you ignore them—that *is* your orientation program. "No orientation" *is* orientation—it's the worst possible type of orientation.

When an organization does this, are the employees going to feel at home? Are they going to think, "Gee, I'm staying here—

> ### The Spurned Celebrity Syndrome
> A particularly painful version of the organizational snub is what I call the "spurned celebrity syndrome."
>
> In this all-too-frequent scenario, the organization, in recruitment mode, woos a hot prospect, perhaps someone with a stellar track record or great qualifications. The prospect is wined, dined, courted, maybe even fawned upon—made to feel like a celebrity.
>
> After a while, the celebrity succumbs to all this flattering attention and accepts the organization's enticing job offer. Then, the new hire arrives, with high expectations of being treated like a celebrity—only to walk straight into the "no orientation" snub … with predictable consequences to the person's morale and commitment.

this is great!"? I suggest the answer to both questions is "highly unlikely."

## Immediate Impact of a Retention-Focused Orientation Program

Orientation programs can be designed to meet any number of objectives—the most common being *time to productivity*. An orientation program that also has *retention* as a main objective must be designed to achieve two immediate and three medium-term goals. (We'll discuss the medium-term goals in the next section.)

> **Key Term**
>
> **Time to productivity** The length of time it takes to get a new employee to the point where he or she can fulfill the requirements of the job autonomously. It will be different for each major job category. For example, a major white goods manufacturer might define time to productivity for a new VP of Sales as the length of time it takes to have him fully in control of his own schedule—making, taking, and running meetings with staff and major clients. Time to productivity for a new production line operative might be the time it takes to get her able to produce 25 units per shift with a less than 0.6% defect rate.

### Escape from Induction

An orientation process designed to be retention-focused must make a clear distinction between *orientation* and *induction*.

Induction (in-processing, form-filling, benefits and compensation details, health and safety instruction) is all about *giving* employees *tools*. Orientation is showing employees what they can *achieve* with the tools. For example, training an employee to use Lotus Notes is induction, while a class on using Lotus Notes to reduce customer call times is orientation.

The key point is this: there's little about induction that's related to retention. Induction is more about *beginning* than *staying*. Concentrating on induction at the expense of orientation undermines your retention activities. Top performers in particular want to get beyond mere induction fairly quickly and on

Asynchronous In this context, any form of training that can take place without the trainer and the employee having to be in the same place at the same time.

CD-ROMs are a good example of asynchronous training. Intranet and Web-based training may or may not be asynchronous, depending on whether or not there's any real-time element (like an Internet chat facility) that requires the trainer and the employee to be online at the same time.

Induction, with its linear, mechanistic elements (choosing 401(k)s, completing medical details, etc.), is ideal for asynchronous delivery. Orientation, with its more individual, "soft skills" emphasis, is not yet well served by the relatively clunky restrictions of asynchronous training design tools.

to orientation. (And, on a more superficial note, induction is mostly boring, while orientation can be fun.)

The more induction you can place on an asynchronous, self-guided platform (CD-ROM, intranet, Web-based), the better. It's worth spending time to find ways to make induction asynchronous, so that more time can be spent on the much more profitable activity of orientation.

Remember: you have three weeks during which your new employees will decide if they feel at home with you and will stay. Don't spend it all showing them how things work (induction); induction emphasizes how "new" they are, that they're not "at home."

## Give Your Employees Permission to Feel at Home

The second immediate impact of an orientation program designed for the retention of top performers should be to give the new employee what he or she needs in order to feel at home as quickly as possible.

Effective orientation helps new hires feel at home by making sure they know four things:

- What is expected of them
- How to add value in your company
- How best to communicate with their colleagues

**Bonding, Not Appraisal**

**Smart Managing**    As we've seen, induction is the in-processing, form-filling, policy-explaining activity that many people automatically think of when they think "orientation." Real orientation, on the other hand, is about enabling your new hires to feel at home—our most important goal. Real orientation quickly dispenses with induction and moves on to help them feel at home.

Too many orientation programs do quite the opposite. By drowning the new employee in huge amounts of information, acronyms, and phrases that he or she cannot possibly understand at that point, they end up *distancing* the employee from the employer.

When this happens, orientation, instead of promoting bonding between the employee and employer, causes the employee to do a cool appraisal, to mentally step back to try to make sense of this flood of information. That appraisal can easily turn to dissatisfaction.

• How to integrate as team players more quickly.

Let's briefly consider these four points.

**Know what's expected of you.** *Orientation:* "We have a strong commitment here to maintaining a work-life balance. Let me show you what that means about working hours in this organization ...."

**Know how to add value.** *Orientation:* "Our major challenge right now is to reduce customer service call response times by 40%. We're expecting you to investigate the technology investment we have to make to achieve that."

**Know how to communicate with others.** *Orientation:* "Here is your divisional organization chart, together with everyone's telephone extensions and e-mail addresses. At lunch today you'll get a chance to meet with the two people to whom you will most often report. We've asked them to talk to you specifically about how best to communicate with them."

**Know how to integrate into the team.** *Orientation:* "This is Jose. He's your assigned 'buddy' for the next three weeks. It's his job to introduce you to everyone you'll be working with closely and to explain how the team interacts."

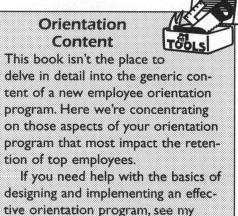

## Length Is Not Important

You will have your own ways of approaching each of the four fundamental points, whether by one-to-one discussions between new employee and manager, handouts, classroom training, or otherwise. In terms of making your employees feel at home, the length and style of your orientation program are not important. What matters are the four points. If your orientation doesn't hit these four points, then it isn't helping your new employees feel at home.

Review your current orientation program content. Which of the four points are covered? How would you score your orientation program on each point using a scale from 1 (pretty poor) to 5 (great)? Which areas need work? Who's going to redesign these elements? When?

## Medium-Term Goals of a Retention-Focused Orientation Program

Getting past induction and helping your employees feel at home are the two immediate goals for a retention-focused orientation program. Achieving both has an obvious and immediate effect on the employees' productivity.

As we said earlier, a retention-focused orientation program also has three medium-term goals:

### Orientation Content

This book isn't the place to delve in detail into the generic content of a new employee orientation program. Here we're concentrating on those aspects of your orientation program that most impact the retention of top employees.

If you need help with the basics of designing and implementing an effective orientation program, see my guide, *The Complete Guide to Orientation and Re-Orientation* (EVNA, 2000), available from Amazon.com or at www.deliverthepromise.com.

1. Acknowledge that "retention starts here."
2. Manage expectations.
3. Encourage cultural integration.

These three goals may not have any immediate impact on productivity or any visible effect on the employees' attitude, but each has a fundamental and vital role in turning your new hires into valued long-term employees. Let's examine each of these in turn.

## Retention Starts Here

In the status-quo employer-employee relationship, orientation programs were an outgrowth of the recruitment function: "Now that we've hired them, I guess we'd better tell them what they need to get on with the job."

As a result, orientation was often restricted to what we've seen is really an induction process—a mechanical explanation of the legislative, compensation, and other company policies necessary to ensure a smooth running of the HR function during the employee's time with the company. Depending on the type of work the new employee would be doing, this induction was sometimes accompanied by on-the-job basic skills training in a sort of "induction plus" program.

Now, with awareness of the importance of retention increasing, the emphasis in orientation is moving, from seeing it as the *end* of the *recruitment* function to seeing it as the *beginning* of the *retention* process. This has considerably broadened the objectives of the average orientation program, to include elements specifically intended to demonstrate the employer's commitment to retaining the employee right from Day 1.

For example, Table 8-1 shows how a mid-sized architectural practice worded its employee orientation program objectives to ensure that retention starts here.

In order to achieve these objectives, the practice designed the following content elements of the orientation program:

- A working session with each employee's manager to establish one- and three-year career goals.
- A presentation from the dean of the practice's corporate university, detailing the personal and career development resources available.
- A session facilitated by a four-year veteran employee, outlining the personal and career development she had achieved during her time with the practice.

| Retention Imperative | Orientation Program Objective |
|---|---|
| Retention starts here | To demonstrate to all employees our commitment to them as their current employer by:<br>• Establishing clear personal and career development goals for a one- and three-year period<br>• Detailing the resources available for the attainment of those goals, and<br>• Providing a mentor-based relationship as a role model for future growth.<br>Our commitment will be demonstrated as coming from the company, senior management, supervisors, and peers equally. |

Table 8-1. "Retention starts here" orientation program objective

• A session launching the employees into the company's formal mentoring program.

**Ask Around**

Here are three steps to help you design orientation program objectives and content that will emphasize to your new hires that "retention starts here":

1. Speak to one or two of your organization's recruiters, one or two supervisors who are responsible for new employees, and, if possible, a senior manager. Ask each of them what message they want to communicate to new employees regarding the organization's commitment to retention. What do they think is the message that's being sent currently?

2. Find out from your new hires as they arrive what they think of your organization's commitment to retention. Speak informally to five employees in your organization who have been hired recently (but more than three months ago). Ask them to think back to when they joined. How did the organization show its commitment to retaining them, if at all? What could the organization have done during orientation to more strongly demonstrate a commitment to retaining them?

3. Use this information to decide how to redesign your orientation program to better demonstrate a commitment to employee retention. How could you use your orientation program to make it clear that "retention starts here"?

### Expectation Management

The second way in which a successful orientation program will improve retention in the medium term is by affirming the new employee's expectations of personal and career development.

As we've seen, high-caliber employees tend to select employers not solely on the basis of the compensation package, but also for the learning and development experience.

During recruitment, your new employees will have heard a lot about what your organization has to offer them in this regard and they will have based their decision to join you largely on those promises and the *expectations* that those promises built. Your orientation program is the first opportunity your new employees have to see how the organization will deliver on its promises. A poor or insufficient orientation program will cause a crisis of expectations that can have fatal consequences for the future of the relationship.

Table 8-2 shows how a database development company worded its employee orientation program objectives to ensure it positively managed new employees' expectations:

| Retention Imperative | Orientation Program Objective |
|---|---|
| Expectation management | This program will ensure that all our employees begin their employment with [us] with realistic working expectations by:<br>• Replicating realistic working conditions as closely as possible<br>• Encouraging debate and discussion about individual expectations over the next 18 months<br>• Pairing of all employees with buddies, and<br>• Mandating attendance by all company recruiters |

Table 8-2. "Employee expectations" orientation program objective

What expectations are your new hires bringing to the organization when they arrive? Speak to the person in charge of your recruitment activities. Find out what "story" recruiters, recruitment ads, your Web site, and other publicly available materials

are giving out about working with your organization.
List the promises that
they're making, implicitly
or explicitly, to prospects.

Using the information
you've gathered, summa-
rize on a sheet of paper
what you think would be
reasonable for a new
employee to expect from
your organization on Day
1. Then answer these questions:

> **What Content
> Would You Use?**   Smart
> Managing
> Flip back to Table 8-1 and
> compare the orientation program
> objective in that table with the pro-
> gram *content* that was used to achieve
> that objective.
>
> Now look at Table 8-2. If this were
> your organization, what orientation
> program *content* would you design to
> achieve that objective?

- Does your orientation program meet or address those
  expectations?
- Are your new employees suffering from a "commitment
  dip" because their expectations are either ignored or
  deflated?
- How might your orientation program fail to live up to your
  new employees' expectations?
- What aspects of the design and content of your orientation program might clash with the promises your new
  employees believe have been made to them?
- Does your orientation program jibe with the description of
  your organization being presented by recruiters and your
  recruiting materials? If not, what remedial action is
  required?
- What implications do your employees' expectations have
  for the redesign and content of your orientation program?

### Cultural Integration

The third way in which your orientation program will help with
retention in the medium term is by accelerating the *cultural
integration* of your new hires.

In addition to an alignment of *expectations*, retention is intimately linked with an alignment of *values* and *goals* between

### Involve the Recruiters

A recruiter's job is difficult in the best of times. Recruiters have to ensure a constant flow of employees to fit every position the organization wishes to fill—and often under tremendous time pressure.

It's not surprising, therefore, that sometimes recruiters will "gild the lily" to get the hire. They'll talk up the organization's strengths, minimize its weaknesses, and (sometimes) completely ignore its failings. While this is understandable from a recruiting perspective, in terms of employee retention it becomes a quietly ticking bomb, ready to explode at some point.

An employee who has been wooed with a less than wholly truthful picture will have expectations that reality will soon burst, with predictable retention effects. And it will happen first during the orientation process.

For this reason it's very important to keep your recruiters and your orientation trainers in the real world. Have them swap jobs occasionally—and, at the very least, make sure every recruiter attends at least one orientation program per quarter. It will help the recruiters stick to the truth if they have to live with the consequences of their sales pitches.

employee and employer. Cultural integration means more than just working as an effective team member (which is essentially a skill that can be taught). Cultural integration represents a voluntary alignment of employer's and employee's visions for what each is trying to achieve.

Your orientation program should therefore do the following:

- Set the bar for the employee by explaining the organization's core vision and values.
- Begin to engage the employee in a discussion about his or her own vision and values, which will be continued in the performance appraisal process (see Chapter 9).

As we've seen so often, at the heart of retention is a *sense of belonging*. No one willingly leaves an environment in which he or she feels at home. Your orientation program is the first (and therefore most important) opportunity to build such a sense of belonging. Get it wrong and the relationship may never recover.

Table 8-3 shows how a global design agency defined its

**Dialogue, Not Monologue**

Achieving this third medium-term goal involves a dialogue between the employer and the employee about each other's vision and values. It's amazing how many orientation programs are straight monologues *at* the employee, rather than a constructive engagement *with* the employee.

Top performers in particular won't appreciate this very much, nor will they benefit from it. You should be designing your program to allow new hires to express what they believe they're bringing to the organization and what they want from the relationship in both the short and long terms.

**Smart Managing**

| Retention Imperative | Orientation Program Objective |
|---|---|
| Cultural integration | By completion of The [XYZ Company] Orientation Program, every partner [company term for "employee"] will be a member of the [XYZ Company] family. |

Table 8-3. "Cultural integration" orientation program objective

commitment to cultural integration. (Notice the absence of *how*'s. This is about *what*. The *how*'s come later.) Their expressed goal is simple, elegant, and sweeping.

To achieve this goal, this organization included the following content in its orientation program. (The following is only an excerpt; there were 16 content elements supporting the objective of cultural integration.)

- An "acronym quiz" to ensure all new employees understood the vocabulary used in the organization.
- A "legends and myths" book was distributed, detailing the many (sometimes apocryphal) stories that had developed about the history and development of the company.
- Buffet lunch over three days, with tables hosted by representatives of senior management.
- A mid-program "town hall" conducted by the CEO.

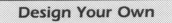

**Design Your Own**

To design your own orientation program content to achieve cultural integration, follow this process.

Speak to five employees in your organization who have been hired recently (but more than three months ago). Ask them:

- In what situations did they feel left out during their first few weeks with the organization?
- What made them feel left out? A lack of knowledge or understanding? About what?
- How did they overcome this sense of exclusion? Did they find information? Did they talk with someone? Did they learn a skill or a vocabulary? Or did they just "tough it out"?

Speak to three managers, supervisors, team leaders, or shift leaders responsible for new employees. Ask them:

- In what situations do they experience new employees failing to appreciate the importance or impact of the organization's cultural or ethical standards?
- What do the employees fail to appreciate? Standards that are required of them? Processes they're expected to follow? Traditions or techniques that are part of "how the organization ticks"?

Look at the responses to your questions. How can the design and content of your orientation bridge these cultural integration issues and prevent similar experiences for future new employees?

- Flowers or other gifts sent to the new employees' significant others at their home address, with a note expressing thanks for their support.

## Developing Cohesive Retention-Focused Orientation Program Content

The two "immediate impact" goals of a retention-focused orientation program—getting past induction and helping your new employees feel at home—are fairly universal to all circumstances. However, not all three medium-term goals of employee retention—

- Begin the retention process immediately.
- Manage expectations.

- Encourage cultural integration.

—are equally important at all times to all organizations.

For some companies, the major cause of dissatisfaction may be mismanaged employee expectations. For others, the real issue may be that it's hard for new employees to feel like part of the team (cultural integration).

It's important to be clear about which aspects of retention really are issues in your organization. Putting emphasis on the *wrong* aspect of retention can be worse than ignoring the issue altogether. Misjudging the climate within your organization and putting processes in place to deal with *cultural integration*, for example, when the issue is really *managing expectations* will confuse your employees and leave them believing that the organization is out of touch and insincere.

To make sure you deal with the right issues, use Table 8-4 to weight the relative importance of each area to your organization.

| Retention Imperative | 1. Not a problem at all—we're completely on top of this. | 2. We only occasionally have a problem with this. | 3. We face this issue fairly regularly. | 4. There is no doubt this contributes to employee dissatisfaction. | 5. People are leaving in droves and this is the reason. |
|---|---|---|---|---|---|
| Retention starts here | | | | | |
| Manage expectations | | | | | |
| Cultural integration | | | | | |

Table 8-4. Prioritizing orientation program imperatives

For each retention imperative you marked as 3, 4, or 5 in Table 8-4, draft an orientation program objective specific to your organization in Table 8-5. Use the examples given in Tables 8-1 and 8-2 as guides.

## Design Specific Orientation Program Content for Each Objective

Finally, for each program objective in Table 8-5, write three specific content elements for your orientation program that will ful-

| Draft an orientation program objective for each retention imperative you marked as 3, 4, or 5. | |
| --- | --- |
| Retention Imperative | Orientation Program Objective |
| Retention starts here | |
| Manage expectations | |
| Cultural integration | |

Table 8-5. Drafting orientation program objectives

fill each objective. Again, use the examples given earlier in this chapter as guides.

## Manager's Checklist for Chapter 8

❏ There's a strong link between retention and effective orientation.

❏ Orientation gives the new employee his or her vital, initial direction.

❏ There's no such thing as "no orientation." In fact, "no orientation" is the worst type of orientation.

❏ It's essential to build an orientation program that focuses on retention.

❏ Retention-focused orientation quickly moves past induction and helps the new employee feel at home.

| Draft three orientation program content modules for each program objective in Table 8-5. | |
|---|---|
| **Retention Imperative** | **Orientation Program Content** |
| Retention starts here | |
| Manage expectations | |
| Cultural integration | |

Table 8-6. Drafting orientation program content

❏ Retention-focused orientation programs emphasize three things in the medium term:

• They acknowledge that "retention starts here."
• They manage expectations.
• They encourage cultural integration.

❏ Your orientation program should contain specific content elements that achieve each of these three objectives.

# The Role of the Manager, Part 1

*First and foremost as a manager your job is to get things done through other people. ...You are paid to manage, not perform every task.*

—Mary Ann Allison
Vice President, CitiCorp

*We do not expect you to follow us all the time, but if you would have the goodness to keep up with us occasionally.*

—Thomas Beecham
Conductor, The London
Philharmonic Orchestra

The key relationship in retention is the relationship between the employee and his or her manager. Get it right and acceptable retention is almost assured. Get it wrong and everything else will count for naught.

In this chapter and the following, we will examine in detail the relationship between the manager and his or her employees, concentrating on those aspects of the relationship that most positively promote retention.

## Onboarding

In the previous chapter, we saw the importance of effective orientation in retaining top performers. But there is only so much an orientation process can achieve for your new employees. As manager, you're responsible for helping your new employees come on board. In particular, there are four areas in which you must take action in order to optimize the effects of the orientation process on retention:

- Acclimation
- Integration
- Dialogue
- Expectation management

### Acclimation

An orientation program can help acclimate a new employee, but for a maximum effect on retention you should also get involved, early on. With your top performers in particular, you should take responsibility for the following aspects of the acclimation process:

> **Key Term**
>
> **Acclimation** The process of helping the new employee become familiar and adjust to his or her new surroundings, ensuring that the employee knows enough about what's going on to feel comfortable and relaxed.

- Clarify the roles and interaction of the management team (i.e., you and your peers).
- Explain interpretations of company policy that will materially impact the employee's "comfort zone" and performance in the early weeks on the job.
- Tell about any department-, division-, or team-specific events, habits, traditions, or other undocumented practices that will materially impact the employee's "comfort zone" and performance in the early weeks on the job.

Let's take an example that we will follow throughout this chapter: Juanita, sales manager, and Joe, the new addition to her sales team.

In welcoming Joe, Juanita takes her usual 30-minute, one-on-one session to explain three things:

- How she and the other Sales VPs work together (including why Henry, VP of the Western Division, sits in on her team meetings, because he has a major client with a large number of plants in Juanita's region).
- Why the company's usual terms of 45 days net are waived for three customers that Joe will be meeting in his first week.
- That there's a tradition among Joe's colleagues on Juanita's team to meet for an hour early on Monday mornings to informally discuss the agenda before that day's divisional sales meeting.

### Integration

Acclimation deals with the *environment*. Integration deals with *people*.

In addition to getting your new employee comfortable with his or her new environment, you must take time to integrate the new employee into the team. Here are some recommendations:

- Walk the new employee around the office, introducing him or her to each person one at a time.
- Set up a conference call with out-of-office employees for initial introductions.
- Have doughnuts delivered to the new employee's desk and call the other employees to gather there at the same time to meet and chat.
- Arrange a social event, like a bowling night, so the new employee and other members of the team have a chance to become acquainted in a social environment.
- Have the new employee stand up and say a few words at a divisional meeting.

### Dialogue

In any relationship, the more open dialogue in the early stages, the longer lasting the relationship. That's true for the relationship between employee and manager. Orientation is notoriously poor at providing opportunities for dialogue; it's most often a monologue *from* the organization *to* the employee. In any case, it's hard to have a dialogue with an organization: you can really dialogue only with another person. As that new employee's manager, you have both the responsibility and the resources to have an effective dialogue with him or her.

> **Party of One?**
>
> If the only "team" for your new employee to meet is you, it's advisable to do at least some of the introductory activities with people in the departments with which the new employee will be interacting most frequently. Avoid overwhelming your new employee, however: your goal is to help him or her become comfortable.

Does this mean that you and your new employee must spend hours together, weeks on end, talking and talking? In most cases, no. Appropriate dialogue will consist of three elements:

- An early discussion regarding the new employee's hopes and aspirations and personal goals for his or her time with the organization.
- The interaction already undertaken to achieve acclimation and integration.
- A period of three to four weeks when you should seek out your new employee at least once a week and discuss any issues or concerns that have arisen.

> **Use All the Tools at Your Disposal**
> *Smart Managing*
>
> Your early dialogue with a new employee need not be all face to face. (Indeed, that may be impossible for any or all of it.) Use all the communication tools at your disposal: telephone, e-mail, and videoconferencing. Many organizations are beginning to use instant messaging to great success, particularly for employees frequently on the move but with access to laptops or PDAs.

### Expectation Management

Your final onboarding responsibility is to help manage your new employee's expectations.

> ### Reality Check
>
> **TRICKS OF THE TRADE** For less experienced, entry-level employees, the 90-day reality check can be fairly fundamental; it often involves a major realignment of their expectations and goals. On the other hand, a 90-day reality check with more experienced employees is often more of a question of nuance, since they're less likely to have come into the job with wildly unrealistic expectations (although it happens!). Nonetheless, this process is still very important. If you're dealing with employees who are at the top of their game, even the smallest tweak of their attitude, commitment, and goals can produce substantial changes in their performance, their sense of "being at home," and therefore their retention.

Most new employees (at any level) take an expectation "dip" about 90 days into their new job. This is usually for two reasons:

1. Their expectations were unrealistically high.
2. The effort of learning associated with the new job—clarifying the job description, learning the acronyms, getting to know the people—tends to exert a gravitational pull on motivation and commitment.

You can materially reduce the impact of point 1 through the dialogue activity outlined above and point 2 through the acclimation and integration activities.

Even so, when your new employee has been on the job about 90 days, it's important to discuss *specifically* his or her short- and long-term expectations, gently helping the employee realign those expectations with the reality that he or she has experienced.

## Setting Goals

With each new employee, you'll begin a process that will be repeated many times throughout that person's career with the organization and that has a major impact on the retention of any employee, especially top performers—setting goals.

Top employees live and die by goals. They strive to excel and need clearly established goals against which to measure their success. An organization that does not provide realistic, specific goals will have great difficulty retaining its top performers.

For these employees, setting goals should achieve three purposes:

**Developing Goal-Setting Skills**

This is not the place for discussing the art and skill of setting goals. We're concentrating on the specific goal-setting needs of top performers and I'm assuming that you understand the underlying principles. However, if you need to brush up on your basic goal-setting skills, I recommend any books by Jim Cairo or Gary Ryan Blair—both excellent communicators on this topic.

1. Ensure that the employee does the necessary tasks of the job.
2. Provide projects that challenge the employee.
3. Provide meaningful work by showing the employee the relevance of the job.

## Set Goals for the Job

The core purpose of setting goals is to ensure that your employee achieves the tasks set out in his or her job description (or otherwise established). This is the most commonly undertaken (and most straightforward) goal-setting activity.

Juanita will begin the goal-setting process with Joe by outlining his sales targets and showing him how to establish his call routine, construct call sheets, and complete his monthly report.

## Set Goals to Challenge

With your best employees, goal setting cannot stop at agreeing how to achieve job-specific tasks. They need to be challenged: prolonged repetition of the same tasks will rapidly lead to boredom and a sense of being underutilized—a sure way to start your top performer on the road to looking elsewhere for a more demanding job. Accordingly, you need to convert *tasks* into *projects* that challenge your employees.

In briefing Joe, Juanita starts by helping him set the first

### Maverick Alert!

With top employees, using goal setting to ensure that they do the required tasks can prove daunting and sometimes tiring. High performers can sometimes see this aspect of setting goals as mundane and boring compared with the other two purposes (providing challenging projects and delivering meaningful work). Also, top performers tend to think that they need little help with this part of the process.

Despite the difficulty, don't ignore this step! It's a mistake to move on to providing challenging projects and delivering meaningful work without first ensuring that your employees achieve their tasks.

year's sales quota as detailed above (task-related goals). She then challenges Joe to achieve at least 15% of that quota from new accounts in the pharmaceuticals industry—an industry in which the company is currently underrepresented. Now Joe has a goal that not only will help the company broaden its sales but also will challenge him more than his basic sales quota.

### Set Goals for Relevance and Meaning

Putting together task-oriented goals and bundling them into challenging projects is good, but not enough to meet the goal-setting needs of top performers. The final step is to ensure that these employees are keenly aware that their work is *relevant*.

### Not Optional!

You should bundle task-oriented goals into challenging projects for *all* of your employees and provide *all* of them with meaningful work, but it may not always be possible. With your best performers, however, these steps in the goal-setting process are not optional. They must be challenged and feel relevant: it's almost always essential to their social and psychological makeup. Don't miss these steps!

Top employees rarely stay for long with an organization where they feel that their work is irrelevant (or insufficiently appreciated—but we'll deal with that point separately). You can help ensure that their work feels meaningful by setting goals that are connected as directly as possible to the core of the business

---

**Doses of Vitamin "C"**

Make sure that your top employees get the opportunity to **Smart Managing** meet a C-level board representative in a town hall, question-and-answer environment at *least* each year, preferably every six months, and ideally once a quarter, to ensure that they have an overview and an understanding of the organization's overall goals and where they fit in.

Use this event as an opportunity to check in with your employees individually about how you and they understand their task and project goals and to clear up any area of concern, ambiguity, or misunderstanding regarding their goals and their strategic importance.

---

operation and the organization's overall strategic objectives.

When Juanita gives Joe his sales quota for the year and challenges him to make at least 15% of that quota from new pharmaceutical accounts, she asks the VP of Marketing to meet with Joe to explain how the sales goal and especially the pharmaceutical goal align with the organization's overall strategy. Joe feels more motivated to work to make his quota and meet the challenge when he understands his role in the big picture.

## Performance Management

After onboarding and setting goals, your next responsibility to your best performers is to ensure that you manage their *performance* related to those goals in a way that promotes retention. As with setting goals, it's important to recognize that performance management is *not* an *optional* step with top employees. (We encourage performance management with *all* employees, if possible.) As we've said frequently, those who perform well *require* effective performance management to excel, thrive, and develop in a way that will keep them with your organization.

How does retention-related performance management differ from any other performance management? Let's look at the retention implications of the three essential elements of performance measurement:

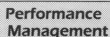

**Performance Management**

Smart Managing This book focuses on performance management in terms of retention. If you need help with the basic principles of performance management, I can strongly recommend *Performance Management* by Robert Bacal (McGraw-Hill, 1999), an esteemed authority on the topic.

- Data collection
- Appraisal
- Feedback

## Data Collection

The first step in any effective performance management process is to collect appropriate data about the employee's performance. This activity may seem routine and innocuous, but it can alienate employees and negatively affect retention if you don't handle it properly.

To minimize possible negative effects, follow these steps in collecting data:

**CAUTION! Ask with Care!** Unless you take care in collecting performance data, some employees can react negatively to what they might perceive as an undue emphasis on the quantitative (e.g., number of sales calls made, experiments performed, patents filed). It may seem to them to be perfunctory, or intrusive if not handled appropriately.

- Tell the employee why you're collecting the information.
- Involve the employee in deciding what relevant data should be collected.
- Ask the employee how best to collect the data.
- As much as possible, have the employee collate the data, not someone else.
- If someone else must collect the data, make sure it's done in a non-judgmental manner. Remember: at this stage you're just gathering information. Appraisal comes later!
- Collect the information in a timely way, not in a rush at the end of the period.

## Appraisal

After collecting the information, the next stage in performance management is the appraisal process. In many organizations,

> ### Get Training
> If you're uncomfortable doing performance appraisals and/or if you tend to do late or cursory performance appraisals or even not at all, think about getting some training.
>
> Considering the importance of the performance appraisal in ensuring that the organization achieves its strategic goals. It's amazing how few managers receive any formal training on the subject. When I finish training sessions on conducting performance appraisals, I'm always amazed at the number of veteran managers who tell me it's their first formal training for appraisals.
>
> You wouldn't let an unqualified mechanic check out your car and you certainly wouldn't accept a medical prognosis from an unqualified doctor. Your employees deserve at least the same consideration when it comes to evaluating their performance and guiding their careers.

this stage is part of the dreaded "annual review"—an activity often postponed and eventually undertaken at the last moment (or even later) by two unenthusiastic participants. That situation is bad enough in terms of helping all employees perform to the best of their potential—but it's terrible in terms of keeping your best employees.

You can make your performance appraisals more effective and more positive—and more likely to keep your employees—by following these three recommendations:

- Get formal training on the importance and conduct of performance appraisals. Top employees find it exceptionally demotivating to be appraised by a manager who cannot do it competently.
- Base your appraisal on the employee's goals (as discussed in the previous section). Those goals should be your focus, not any particular concern you might have at the time. Those goals will help you avoid a "Well, how do you think this year went?" generic review. Top performers *want* to be evaluated according to their specific goals: it's how they know they have succeeded or failed. When you don't do so, you decrease the value of setting goals.
- Make your appraisal timely. The longer you wait after the period under review, the more time you allow any

problems to persist and the harder it becomes to remember specifics. Delays also undermine the credibility of the goal-setting process for the future.

### Feedback

The final step of the performance management process is giving the employee feedback on the appraisal. This is important for all employees, for their personal and career development, but especially for top performers—and essential for retaining them.

Here's how to make the most of performance management feedback:

- **Make it specific.** Don't just sum up the period under review. Effective feedback is a detailed, step-by-step review of each key goal. Use an overview only to start and finish the feedback session.
- **Make it positive.** High performers respond well to positive reinforcement, less well to negative criticism. It's important to give feedback on failures as well as successes, but do it constructively to help them improve their performance or they will eventually leave.
- **Make it challenging.** Don't just tell your employees what happened and how you feel about it; challenge them with a specific outcome that you would like to see. If you're discussing a success or a strength, reinforce the

---

**Peek Inside**

**Smart Managing**    Top performers need communication and feedback. Many top employees appear self-contained, perhaps difficult to approach. Don't be fooled by the cover! Peek inside and you'll see a person who needs even more communication and feedback than other employees.

Feedback is essential to the top performers' internal process for benchmarking against their own exacting standards and goals—their single most important motivator. When dealing with top performers, think of feedback not as something that will change their performance directly, but as something they'll use themselves to change their performance.

feedback with suggestions for building on that success
or strength. If you're discussing a weakness or a failure,
give suggestions for remedying the weakness or preventing such failures.

- **Make it practical.** Employees respond better to feedback they can use. Vague comments like "I think you
  could do better" or "I want to see a large increase in
  your sales activity" don't cut it. Be practical and, if possible, give them tools they can use.

Juanita is reviewing the first quarter performance of Joe,
her top sales performer. He has only just failed to make his
overall sales quota, but has greatly exceeded the 15% of
the quota for new accounts in the pharmaceutical industry.

Juanita congratulates Joe on his performance and then
mentions that the sales average of his new pharmaceutical
accounts is only 80% of the overall sales average for the
company. She points out that if Joe can squeeze a slightly
higher initial sale from the new pharmaceutical accounts,
he will readily hit his quota.

Notice that Juanita has given feedback that's *specific, positive, challenging,* and *practical.*

## Growth and Development

You're responsible for providing growth and development
opportunities for all of your employees. However, it's especially
important to do so for your high performers. Survey after survey has shown that such opportunities are essential for retaining
these employees.

There are three factors to consider in providing growth and
development opportunities for your employees, particularly
your top performers:

- Make the opportunities specific to the individual.
- Provide associated training and experience.
- Present the opportunities in a way that will
  maximize the chance that the employees will
  take advantage of them.

## Work the Contract

**Smart Managing** The "status quo" employment contract stated that so long as the employee continued to do good work, the employer would provide employment and reasonable compensation. There was no mention of growth or development there.

By contrast, the "new" employer-employee contract can be readily summarized as "You continue to develop me and give me growth opportunities and I will stay here."

If you're not providing such opportunities, you can kiss your best employees goodbye—and sooner rather than later.

## Individual Growth Plans

The first step is to develop an individual growth plan for each employee, or at least each of your top performers. An *individual growth plan* (IGP)—also known as an *individual development plan* (IDP) or an *individual training plan* (ITP)—is a concept that uses discussion and joint decisions by the employee and his or her manager (possibly with input from a mentor and/or a coach) to determine the specific developmental experiences necessary for the employee to meet his or her career aspirations and (if mutually compatible) associated organizational goals.

Each IGP is specific to the needs of the individual and the organization. One IGP might emphasize skills training, another might focus on obtaining a specific qualification, and yet another might feature geographical or functional exposure. There is no standard content for an IGP: the main driver is the employee's willingness and capacity to learn and grow.

## Key Term

**Individual growth plan (IGP)** A set of specific developmental experiences determined by an employee and his or her manager to be necessary for the employee to meet his or her career aspirations and compatible, associated organizational goals. Also known as an *individual development plan* (IDP) or an *individual training plan* (ITP).

Such plans are becoming more commonplace in organizations. Unfortunately, they often suffer from the same weaknesses as the performance review process—too little, too late. To ensure that top employees benefit most from their

IGPs, each IGP must be:

- Specific to the employee.
- Relevant to the employee's particular needs and developmental requirements.
- Timely.

Design the IGP to fit the employee, not just the organization. And don't wait until the employee expresses dissatisfaction with his or her growth opportunities; at that point it will be less effective—and maybe not enough to keep that person around. It's not enough just to provide opportunities; you should anticipate that your better employees will want and expect them.

> **Finding Templates**
>
> If your organization does **TOOLS** not have a formal IGP process, set up an informal process with at least your top employees. To get started, fire up your favorite search engine and key in "individual development plan." When I did it (using Google), the top 10 results contained no fewer than seven great templates for such plans.

## Training and Experience

After designing and agreeing on the IGP with the employee, your next responsibility is to ensure that the employee gets the training and experiences specified in the IGP.

It's exceptionally frustrating for employees to go to the trouble of discussing their personal and career goals and what they want to achieve, only to find that their needs, despite being set out in an IGP, are simply ignored or are downgraded because of time or money or other priorities. To be frank, it's better not to construct an IGP than to raise the employee's expectations by starting down this route and then dash them by neglecting to follow through.

## Convenience

It's not always the employer's fault when IGPs fall by the roadside. It's not at all unusual for employees to help develop an IGP and then fail to take some or all of the opportunities offered. There are

> ⚠️ **CAUTION!**
>
> ### Plan Ahead
>
> For larger organizations with major investments in on-site learning, corporate universities, and a tradition and budget for employee development, the concept of an IGP is usually a straightforward overlay on an existing developmental structure.
>
> For the opposite reasons, this is an area where many small and mid-sized organizations fall down. An IGP program is set up (with the best intentions in the world), employees are engaged and become excited at the prospect that their employers will help them with career and personal development, and then, when the crunch comes, it's just not effective or efficient or possible to send the employee to that conference or let her take that class or let him study for that qualification. This is a short trip to disillusionment and retention difficulties. If you're going to start an IGP program, make sure you have both the budget and the senior management support to follow through.

many reasons, including apathy and "playing the organizational game." But with top employees, the issue is usually a simple one of logistics: "I just never got around to it" is the most common excuse given by top performers for not taking advantage of their IGP opportunities.

You can help avoid such failures by taking three steps when designing the IGP:

- Establish the implementation dates at the start. The rule should be "This doesn't go into the IGP unless the employee schedules the implementation time there and then."
- Support the decision. Your overt support is crucial to success with the IGP. If the employee thinks you're in any way unsupportive or unimpressed by the IGP (either in concept or with regard to specific contents), he or she may just let it slide.
- Follow up with reminders. Reinforce both of the steps above with a simple reminder system. A scheduled e-mail reminder or telephone call at an appropriate time will encourage the employee to take action.

## Providing a Buffer

By their nature, top employees appear on the organizational "radar screen" more than other employees. They're discussed at management meetings, involved in decision-making, chosen for committees, stopped in corridors, included in e-mail circulation lists, volunteered for extracurricular activities, and so on.

All of this is flattering (and, in many cases, helpful and positive), but the cumulative effect can be unproductive (for both the organization and the employees) and, at the extreme, claustrophobic for the employees. Interruptions and distractions will ultimately cause the employees to lose their focus. For top performers, this usually causes a sense of being unfulfilled and, ultimately, a feeling of failure. Thus, attention that begins with the desire to involve and include employees can end with losing them entirely.

It's essential to monitor your top performers' interactions with senior management (and anyone else who can impose on your employees) and to protect your employees from being overwhelmed, swamped, or distracted. As a manager, you're responsible for ensuring an environment in which all of your employees can work to the best of their abilities—and that includes protecting your top performers against those who would take their time and energy.

**Beware of the Peter Principle**

This is a variant of the Peter Principle. You're likely familiar with the concept, described by Laurence J. Peter in *The Peter Principle* (William Morrow, 1969), that employees who prove competent in the tasks assigned to them get promoted, until they reach positions where they're no longer competent—and they tend to stay there.

Top employees who attract attention may find that their performance suffers because they're less able to focus their time and energy on their jobs. It's up to you to help them perform to their potential.

## Politics

The first (and, sadly, most prevalent) area in which you must take action is in providing a buffer from the extremes of internal politics. Although it's never possible (or desirable) to completely isolate employees from the effects of company politics, the "radar screen" effect discussed earlier will mean that your top performers, left unprotected, will get sucked into political wrangles more frequently than most employees.

You must act as a lightning rod where possible, taking responsibility for internal political issues rather than allowing them to affect your employees and their performance.

> At a monthly VP sales meeting, one of Juanita's colleagues asks for a detailed report on all of Joe's meetings with pharmaceutical companies. He explains that his detailed knowledge of the pharmaceutical industry can help Juanita review Joe's activity. Juanita strongly suspects that her colleague is grandstanding for the benefit of the COO, who's sitting in on the meeting that day. She thinks that her colleague is unlikely to read the report and that compiling it would not only waste Joe's time, but also confuse and demotivate him. With the help of her technically proficient assistant, she cuts and pastes from Joe's weekly reports and sends the result off to her colleague. As suspected, she hears no more about it.

## Resources

The second major "buffer" role you must play on behalf of all of your employees, and particularly your top employees, is to provide resources, ensuring that your employees have what they need to do their jobs.

Managing top performers is like being in charge of the pit crew in Formula One racing: when the car comes into the pit, your job is to find out what's needed, take care of it, and get the car back into the race as quickly as possible. When employees have to ask for a necessary resource and then "idle" while waiting for it, that disrupts their work, hurts their productivity, and undermines their motivation. That's bad for any employee—but even more so for your top performers.

> ### Give Them What They Need!    **⚠ CAUTION! ⚠**
> Many managers feel that their responsibility for providing
> resources to their employees reduces them to playing
> the role of the employees' assistant. This is a critical misunderstanding.
>
> As stated earlier, it's a manager's basic responsibility to ensure an
> environment in which all of his or her employees can work to the
> best of their abilities. That environment includes resources.
>
> As Brad Humphrey and Jeff Stokes state in *The 21st Century Supervisor*
> (Jossey-Bass, 2000), "To keep employees on track and performing at
> optimum levels, you will be required to provide employees with all the
> different things they need to accomplish their tasks." And they devote a
> chapter in their book to "resource management skills"—"Giving Your
> Employees What They Need to Succeed." It's as simple as that.

## Accountability

Finally, in acting as a buffer for your top employees, you must
keep accountability from "leaking" to an unacceptable level.
Another aspect of the "radar screen" phenomenon, here's how
it goes.

You've got an employee whose performance is beginning to
attract the attention of senior management. Either because
she's costing more than other employees (top performers don't
come cheap) or because of the prominent role she's playing in
helping the organization achieve its strategic goals, the CEO
decides he'd like your top performer to "pop in from time to
time" to keep him apprised of how things are going. Over a
period of time, the "pop-ins" turn into regular meetings, during
which the CEO is coaching, mentoring, and/or appraising the
performance of your employee.

This process will ultimately lead to one of two things:

- You're gradually supplanted as manager of this top performer.
- The top performer becomes confused and distracted by
  reporting to two managers.

Either way, this "accountability leak" has a negative effect
on retention. To keep such leaks from developing, you must

hold the line on a clear, unambiguous accountability and reporting structure. If any members of senior management are interested in any of your employees, it's up to you—and not your employees—to keep them apprised.

## Manager's Checklist for Chapter 9

❏ The relationship between you and your top employees is vital for retaining those employees.

❏ You're responsible for completing the onboarding process for all of your new employees, but particularly for top performers.

❏ You must set realistic, challenging, and relevant goals for your top employees.

❏ You must implement a realistic, challenging, and relevant performance appraisal process.

❏ You must design and implement an individual growth plan for each employee.

❏ You must act as a buffer between any of your employees and other managers.

# The Role of the Manager, Part 2

*Who must account for himself and others must know both.*

—George Herbert, 1593-1633
English clergyman and poet

*Your job is not to criticize your employees, but to critique them.*

—Andrew Grove, CEO, Intel Corp.

As stated in the preceding chapter, the key relationship in retention is the relationship between the employee and his or her manager. In this chapter, we'll continue examining that relationship in terms of the aspects that most positively promote retention.

## The Manager as Company Representative

In the last chapter, we saw that the manager must act as a buffer between senior managers (and other influencers) and the employees. The manager must also act as a representative of the company to the employees.

**Representative, Not Official**

Note that it's your job to *rep-resent* the organization, not necessarily to act as an *official* of the organization. The difference is between *power* and *responsibility*. You may or may not be a company official, with the power to make decisions and set policy, but you're *always* a representative, with the responsibility to properly represent the decisions and policies of the organization.

**Mission**

The first area in which you must represent the organization is in integrating the organization's *mission* into the goals and activities of your top employees.

That mission may be written or not, but if the organization has a clear understanding of its overall goals (which it should!), it's imperative that you integrate that mission into your interactions with your top employees. Otherwise there's a danger that they may begin slowly drifting from the organization's key strategic objectives, resulting eventually in a sense of "disconnect" between the employees and the organization. That, as we've seen, is one of the underlying reasons why top performers leave—a sense of irrelevance.

**Key Term**

**Mission** The goals of an organization, as expressed in the *mission statement*, usually succinct and with a long-term time horizon.

Here's an example—the mission statement of Peet's Coffee & Tea: "Growth without compromise: Peet's will grow aggressively, providing more customers every day the opportunity to enjoy the finest coffee and tea in the world, shipped fresh within 24 hours of order."

**Values**

The second area in which you must represent the organization is in upholding the organization's values (which may or may not be contained in a *values statement*).

It's clearly important that all employees work in accordance with the organization's core values—and the more strongly held those values are, the more important compliance with them becomes. Top performers are often individuals with their own strong core values; the alignment of the employees' core values

---

**Values statement** A written summary of those values that are "core" to the organization—values that cannot be abrogated in pursuing the mission. In its values statement, an organization is saying, "We want to attain our mission, but not at all costs: here is the *way* in which we will attain our goals."

Here is the values statement of Peet's Coffee and Tea:
- Supply only the freshest, highest quality coffee and tea;
- Maintain exemplary employee relations and training;
- Encourage life-long customer relationships;
- Remain the source of coffee knowledge;
- Be ethical and socially responsible.

---

and the organization's core values is of paramount importance to long-term retention.

### Culture

The third way in which you must represent the organization to all of your employees is in communicating the organization's underlying culture. This is more difficult to nail down, because culture involves much more amorphous concepts than mission or values. You must communicate *how* the organization works, using examples such as the following:

> **Write It Down**
>
> If your organization's core values aren't formally written down, but you know them from experience, write down what you think those core values are; it will help you communicate them clearly to your top employees. If you have any doubts about what you've written ("Are we 'aggressive' or are we merely 'persistent'? Do we put customer service above employee satisfaction or the other way around?"), talk it over with some of your senior colleagues. Who knows? You may prompt the organization to produce a formal values statement!

- Does the organization value face time or is e-mail the preferred method of communication?
- What is the organization's approach to work-life issues? Are employees expected to work 80-hour weeks without complaining or is there a push to make sure employees go home at night?

- What about parking spaces and cafeteria seating? Is everything rigidly hierarchical or is the atmosphere more casual and collegial?

These and a hundred other indicators constitute the organization's culture. It's part of your job to ensure that your employees understand and work with that culture.

This is actually an extension of the manager's responsibility (discussed in the preceding chapter) to convey enough about the organization's culture to ensure that new employees are able to fit in well and make a quick start. Here we're discussing the responsibility of the manager for ensuring that employees understand and comply with the organization's culture.

## How to Do It

So how do you ensure that your employees are aligned with the organization's mission, values, and culture? You can't really call in each of your employees for a regular "culture checkup," so here are some tips on managing the culture compliance issue more diplomatically:

1. Discuss values early, before hiring if possible. Most top performers can adapt to an organization's mission and culture, but are less flexible when it comes to values that don't correlate with their own.

**TRICKS OF THE TRADE**           **Think Compliance**

Some managers are uncomfortable with the word "compliance" in such matters as mission, values, and culture. To them the word smacks of heavy-handed, authoritarian attitudes. Fair enough. If you don't like the word, feel free to substitute another of your own choosing, such as "understanding" or "alignment."

But in my experience organizations that are serious about achieving their mission using their values and with their culture treat those issues as seriously as any other issue requiring compliance, such as regulatory or health and safety issues. And rightly so. If it's important to the organization to comply with health and safety regulations, how much more important is it to maintain the integrity of its values and culture in pursuing its mission?

2. Build mission into the goals you set. Make sure your top performers' goals are aligned with the organization's mission. Use the tools in the previous chapter (under "Setting Goals") to make sure when you meet with each of your employees to set goals that they understand the mission and its implications for their activities.
3. Keep a "culture checklist." Most of us aren't consciously aware of organizational culture; it's like the organizational air we breathe—there, but invisible. Improve your chances of communicating your organizational culture clearly by keeping a "culture checklist" where you note down specific instances of how the culture works.
4. Work backwards from functional needs. Use the functional interaction with your best performers to retro-engineer a mission, values, and culture check-in. For example, if you're dealing with a sales team, you might use a major account review to ask questions like these:
   • "How does servicing this client help us meet our overall mission?"
   • "Are we servicing this client in keeping with our underlying values?"
   • "How does our organizational culture impact how we service this client?"

## The Manager as Leader

In retaining top employees, it's very important for you to be a leader. The topic of leadership is so important that many management books would lead you to believe that leadership is all there is to management or that management is merely a subset of leadership.

Actually, the two are separate functions, which may or may not be connected, depending on the individual manager-employee relationship. Management at its lowest level—supervision—requires limited leadership. At the top—at C-level (CEO, COO, CFO, and so on)—management can often be 80% to 90% leadership.

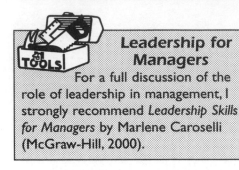

**Leadership for Managers**

For a full discussion of the role of leadership in management, I strongly recommend *Leadership Skills for Managers* by Marlene Caroselli (McGraw-Hill, 2000).

In dealing with top employees, leadership is a delicate matter, because those employees have at least some leadership qualities. Leading top performers is more a question of "Try this" than "Chaaaarge!" The best employees have their own agendas, they want to meet their own goals, and they aren't always great when asked to hook their star to someone else's.

There are, however, three areas in which high performing employees typically respond positively to leadership:

- When they're encouraged to set stretch goals
- When they need a broader perspective for making decisions
- When they're encouraged to think "outside the box"

### Stretch Goals

As strange as it may seem, top performers are not great at setting stretch goals for themselves. This is the flip side of their tremendous ability to focus on operational goals.

**Key Term**

**Stretch goal** A goal that exceeds the established operational goals for a particular person, organization, or event, a goal that extends people's abilities.

As an example, take a top sales rep meeting with her manager to set goals for the incoming year. After discussing overall objectives and agreeing on clear sales targets, she'll usually adopt those targets as if they were written in blood. There is no question but that she will attain her sales target. There's no alternative: "failure is not an option." She carries the target around in her head and benchmarks every sales call, every conversation, every meeting, and every event against her absolute resolution to meet that target. She mentally tallies every sale against that goal until she can say, "Done!"

Now, her manager brings up the concept of a stretch goal, something further out there. How does this sales star react? She thinks, "Oh, did we get it wrong the first time? So this is the new target now?"

Top performers don't need stretch goals to motivate them to hit a higher target. To them, targets are targets. A stretch goal is just a new target—and a statement that the first target was wrong.

Does this mean that stretch targets have no value with top performers? Absolutely not. The difference is in how they are used. For most employees, stretch goals are a *quantitative* stretch—usually "Do more of the same or do it faster." For top employees, stretch goals should be a *qualitative* stretch—"I want you to do this better, more efficiently."

You'll recall our example from the last chapter:

> Juanita, after setting Joe's sales target with him, has chal-
> lenged Joe to obtain 15% of his sales from new accounts in
> the pharmaceuticals industry. She also asks Joe to pioneer
> a new online data-sharing system she's thinking of imple-
> menting for all of her employees, by recording and sharing
> all his sales data on the corporate intranet. This will involve
> Joe in mastering new skills and in working with the
> intranet, something he's not wholly comfortable with. For
> Joe, the sales target is his goal, the pharmaceutical ele-
> ment is a challenge, and the intranet is a stretch.

In the preceding chapter, we discussed the need to chal-lenge top employees. The difference between a challenge and a stretch is one of *comfort*. A top employee will usually relish a challenge (if not actually *need* one), while a stretch should make the top employee *uncomfortable*.

Setting a challenge is *management*. Selling a stretch goal is *leadership*!

## Decision Making

The second area in which top employees appreciate strong leadership is in making tough decisions. These employees are effectiveness personified: they know how to reach their goals (make a sale, complete an audit, file a patent, design a product) and they strive relentlessly to do so. They have a "performance perspective": when something out of the ordinary comes up, they usually perceive it as an obstacle in their way to achieving those goals. As a result, decision making by top performers is often one-dimensional ("I'll choose whatever solution gets me closer to my goals") or ruthless ("I don't care what your needs are; just get out of my way") or both.

**Ruthless Equals Retention Problem** When a top performer consistently, ruthlessly removes all obstacles to achieving his or her goals, isolation from colleagues and others in the organization will eventually follow. With the resulting decrease in communication, the employee will become even more inflexible. Eventually the divergence will become so great that separation from the organization is inevitable.

Your retention of top performers is directly linked to how well you help them make good decisions.

An employee whose approach to making decisions is consistently ruthless will cause major retention issues in the long run. Those decisions will show the extent to which the employee is unlike others on the team and naturally lead to alienation.

You can help your top performers with their decision-making skills by doing the following:

- **Model good decision-making behavior.** When you make a decision, don't "black box" it: make your thought process and your reasoning for the decision transparent. Explain your thinking to your top performers.
- **Involve them in your decision-making.** When you have key decisions to make, even if you don't think you need any help, get your top performers into the process. Help them learn to see a decision from all angles, not just the "performance perspective."
- **Set up checks and balances.** Make sure you have warning mechanisms in place that alert you when your top performers are making decisions that significantly affect oth-

ers. The simplest system is just to make sure other people
alert you when they are likely to be significantly impacted
by a top performer's decision. This is not to suggest that
you put in place a network of snoops and snitches! Deal
with decision making openly and transparently. Just make
sure that in the case of large, significant decisions, your
employees have a safety net that alerts you to help them
examine the widest impact of those decisions.

- **Put on "training wheels."** For a while, work with your top
  employees when they're making material decisions, in a
  collegial collaboration. After they've learned how to consider and assess all factors and potential effects in making decisions, you can ease off on the decision-making
  oversight.
- **Support their decisions.** The more you support quality
  decisions and reinforce good decision-making behavior,
  the more your top performers will develop the habit of
  making "good" decisions.

### Outside the Box

Thinking outside the box is an internalized version of the decision-making issue. The best employees are often experts at
thinking outside the box in order to attain their functional goals,
but much less so when it comes to non-operational matters.
Again, this is the flip side of their sharp focus on their

**Welcome to Tech World**

During the dot-com boom, I spent a lot of time working with
top employees in the tech world—predominantly programmers and
engineers. Most of them could overcome the most complicated technical problems and write code that would make a computer do almost
anything. However, when even the simplest issues arose "outside the
box," like fund raising or employee supervision or even just docu-
menting what they were doing, their creative juices seemed to freeze.
And some of these people were genuine, certified geniuses. More
often than not, as the organization matured and became less flexible
and therefore less capable of dealing with such idiosyncrasies, the top
employees simply left.

own targets: bring something else into the picture and there's often a "deer in the headlights" reaction.

As with making decisions, you must take responsibility for helping your employees think outside the box about issues that are not related to their functional goals. Here are some suggestions:

- **Hold regular "What's going on in your world?"** meetings. These meetings should have only one rule: the employees can talk *only* about work issues that are not directly related to their functional goals. This will help unearth issues requiring outside-the-box thinking.
- **Give each top performer a "buddy."** A very successful response to this issue has been to assign a "buddy" to look out for the top employee and help him or her deal with non-operational issues. This can be a great training ground for younger high-potential employees who get to interact with a top performer and add value at the same time.
- **Build a "parking lot."** Set up a notice board (physical or electronic—whatever works for you) where top performers can simply post a message regarding an issue that's bothering them. Encourage everyone to contribute suggestions and advice. You may well be able to encourage and develop a peer review process that will enable your top employees to help each other.

## The Manager as Work-Life Balance Indicator

This point is somewhat connected to the previous point: top performers need help in achieving work-life balance and their manager needs to help them do it. Burnout serves no interest and certainly hurts retention.

There are three particular ways in which you can help ensure that your employees are maintaining a healthy balance between work and recreation:

- Set the right conditions.
- Monitor key relationships.

- Enforce sensible milestones.

## Set the Right Conditions

It's hard for any employees to achieve work-life balance if the atmosphere in which they work militates against it at every step. You should ensure that the conditions are right to encourage all of your employees to achieve an appropriate balance by adopting appropriate policies.

**Preventing Burnout**
A great Web site to help with work-life balance issues is www.employersforwork-lifebalance.org.uk. This site contains case studies, resources, benchmarking, and even materials to help build an internal case for investing in work-life balance initiatives. It's a "must-visit" for anyone interested in keeping employees from burning out at an early stage.

A necessary first stage is to set out in writing balanced work-life policies and then enforce adherence to them. (As we'll see in a moment, however, that alone is not enough.)

What areas should you cover in your work-life policies? Your organizational culture will dictate the exact contents, but your policies should cover the following as a minimum:

- **Flexible working:** Set clear guidelines for flexible working opportunities. (Include a simple application process to make sure people take the next step.)
- **Leave/vacation:** Clarify annual vacation allowance and the policies surrounding maternity leave, time off for sabbaticals, study leave, unpaid leave, and any other variations you may provide.
- **Employee support:** Detail any support you provide for education, child care, loans, transportation, special equipment, or anything else for your employees.

## Monitoring Relationships

You can set down clear guidelines, but it's almost impossible to oversee every employee's activity and check if he or she is taking advantage of the support available. You need a quick way to assess if your employees are maintaining a reasonable balance, without micro-managing the process. There are three ways to monitor your employees:

- **You:** Take a reality check once a month or so. Does this employee seem overly stressed or unusually touchy? If so, it's time to do more to enforce some work-life balance.
- **Significant Other:** Have an event once a quarter to which significant others are invited (a barbecue, bowling, a ball game, or whatever). Mingle with those significant others and, believe me, if any of your employees are not maintaining a reasonable work-life balance, you'll soon hear about it!
- **Colleagues:** Hard-core overachievers will find ways to hide their problem from those around them. However, it's hard to do so for long. Watch and ask how your best employees are relating to their colleagues (to whom they're exposed for the longest time) to identify employees who are covering up a work-life imbalance.

> ⚠️ **CAUTION!**
>
> ## Don't Snoop!
> Please note that I am not advocating that you snoop on your employees. Snooping is when you surreptitiously sneak around trying to find out what's going on. You must deal with work-life issues openly and transparently: tell your employees what you'll be doing to help them maintain a reasonable balance. They'll thank you for it.

### Setting Milestones

In addition to monitoring relationships, you can put in place "balance milestones" that can be checked almost automatically. Set quantifiable milestones that can be collated and scanned easily for trends that will indicate a possible problem with work-life balance.

As with setting policies, the milestones you set will vary depending on organizational and employee needs, but here are some examples:

- Hours worked per week, month, and quarter.
- Hours worked outside normal working hours per week, month, and quarter.

- Miles traveled per week, month, and quarter.
- Meetings held per week, month, and quarter (a frequent sign of work-life unbalance).
- Cups of coffee consumed per week, month, and quarter.
- Make sure to investigate both spikes *and*

**Trends, Not Numbers**

**Smart Managing**

Your milestones should have timelines. What matters is not the absolute numbers; top performers will always rack up high numbers for all of the milestones. You need to track *trends* over time and watch for any sharp *spikes* or *dips*. If a spike or dip is not explicable for operational reasons (for example, the end of the financial period or a push to get a new product out the door), then find out why it happened.

dips in the milestones you choose. Either one indicates a possible work-life balance issue.

## Managing Departing Employees and Alumni

A little-acknowledged responsibility of the manager of top performers is to manage their exit from the organization.

You will recall that one of the pillars of the new employer-employee relationship is an acceptance that the employee will leave the organization eventually. You should no longer be thinking, then, in terms of *losing* top performers, but rather of accepting the inevitable—and even encouraging them to move on when the time is right.

### Manage the Exit

A well-managed "separation" from the organization will reap retention benefits for the organization in the long run in three ways:

- It will attract other high performers. A top employee who leaves the organization in good shape and in a healthy manner will become an evangelist for that organization, spreading the word about what a great employer you are. And guess who these people bump into a lot? Yep— other top performers.

**The Multiplier Effect**

TRICKS OF THE TRADE

In my experience, a well-managed exit of one high performing individual will bring two or three referrals of other talented employees into the organization over a period of around three years.

Conversely, from my experience (and probably yours, too), a badly handled separation is likely to ensure that the employee will tell about 50 to 60 people never to darken your door.

Treat departing top employees well—even the math tells you it's the right thing to do!

- It will help retain current employees. Generosity about separation terms, helping the employee leave in an orderly manner, and praising the employee for his or her contribution will make current employees feel good about the organization and will positively impact employee retention.
- It will make your managers better people. Managers who handle separations well are for obvious reasons more at peace with themselves, more confident, and better at their jobs than those who react negatively. As we've already seen, good managers positively impact employee retention.

### Keep in Touch

Top performers rarely stop being top performers—and the employee who leaves the organization today could be returning

**Don't Play the Blame Game**

CAUTION!

I've worked with organizations that had such a warped notion of employee loyalty that I've actually witnessed them publicly flail departing employees for alleged disloyalty. Then the employees, once they're out the door, are bad-mouthed among the other employees and are blamed for just about anything wrong that happens.

I've never understood this attitude that if leaving the organization is made as unpleasant as possible, employees will be too terrified to leave. What sort of morale and productivity does that breed? Well, I've worked with organizations with this attitude often enough to know the answer: terrible!

Don't do it.

**Follow Your Alumni**

The approach of encouraging top performers to move on when the time is right and leaving the door open for them to return is particularly effective for younger, homegrown "hotshots." An employee that you've developed internally will reach a point when he or she will need to move on for personal and career development. After all, no matter how great your organization is, a top employee will eventually need to see how other organizations work and learn some new tricks. In any case, natural curiosity will cause him or her to look around sooner or later.

Many younger hotshots find out eventually that "there's no place like home" and, after taking a few years out, they'll often think about returning. So, keep the door open—and keep in touch.

tomorrow. Encouraging former employees to return is a rapidly growing method of promoting retention. It produces two specific retention-related benefits:

- **A bigger recruitment pool.** If you maintain an open door policy for ex-employees and keep in touch with them regularly, you've in effect opened a new channel for recruiting top performers.
- **A longer average stay.** Employees who return typically stay longer the second time around. They know what to expect and they assimilate and acclimate more quickly.

### Involve Alumni

You can go beyond simply keeping in touch with high performers who leave. Why not consider asking them to remain involved in some way? When you can keep top alumni involved (speaking at management retreats or other employee events, serving as mentors for younger employees, or just attending an occasional social event), that involvement delivers all the benefits detailed above. And there's one additional, important retention benefit: it minimizes "collateral losses."

If your employees can continue to interact with their departed colleagues, it minimizes the separation distress and radically reduces collateral losses.

**Collateral losses** Employees who leave the organization in the weeks or months after an employee leaves, whether because they worked closely with the person, depended on him or her for assistance, or "just because the place isn't the same" without the person. Top performers, when they leave, tend to cause more collateral losses than do other employees.

## Leverage Alumni Contacts

Top employees who've left an organization that they come to view as their "alma mater" are powerful retention tools, in that they can recommend your organization to others as a good place to work and they can help reduce collateral losses by remaining in contact with the organization.

But that's not all. Here are some more ways to leverage alumni contacts:

- Have alumni call potential top performers holding job offers from you and answer any questions they may have about joining the organization.
- Ask alumni to take part occasionally in orientations of new employees to help with expectation management.
- Ask alumni to mentor your younger high performers.
- Provide alumni with recruiting materials to distribute at industry events.

### Mark Mentors Maggie

When I owned a graphic design firm, my top designer left to set up his own shop. I was prepared for Mark to leave—we'd talked about it for a while—but my main concern was with Maggie, Mark's natural successor. Maggie had worked with Mark for two years and I knew she was exceptionally nervous about stepping into Mark's shoes.

We cut a deal for Mark to come back regularly (on a sliding scale, starting at one day a week, reducing to one afternoon a month, over a six-month period) to mentor Maggie into her new role. It worked very well. Maggie developed her confidence (she eventually bought the firm from me) and Mark received some income that was very useful in the early days of his new business. In addition, the two firms continued to collaborate on larger projects for many years to come.

---

**Get Virtual**

The single, simplest tool for keeping in touch with your alumni is a "shared space" on your corporate intranet or the Internet. This is a closed, password-protected site that only your alumni (or anyone else you authorize) can access. You can use it to send newsletters, plan and schedule events, have discussion boards, and even post photographs.

Colleges and universities are already doing this to a great extent; you can see hundreds of examples by keying "alumni intranet" into your favorite search engine.

To start an alumni intranet, you don't need any technical skills. Just look at the "point and click" tools provided by sites such as www.intranets.com or www.communityzero.com.

---

- Ask alumni to talk with current employees who are feeling unhappy and considering leaving.
- Invite alumni to speak once a year to your top performers as a group and to facilitate a discussion on how they can achieve their personal goals in the year to come.
- Ask alumni to join your top performer retention working group as an "outside director."
- In all of these cases, involving someone outside the organization has much more credibility than enlisting someone currently employed by the organization.

## Manager's Checklist for Chapter 10

❏ You must act as a representative of the organization with your top employees.

❏ Leadership is a key role that you must play.

---

**What About Their Current Employers?**

Won't your alumni's current employer throw a fit at this degree of involvement? Well, yes—if you ask any one ex-employee to do all of the suggested tasks. But not if you spread the requests around a group of alumni, so no one person is overburdened. You'll find that this process is self-filtering: the alumni won't agree to do more than either they or their employers would be comfortable with.

❏ Leading top performers is as much an art as a science.

❏ It's your responsibility to ensure that your top employees have a reasonable work-life balance.

❏ Manage the departure of your top employees appropriately.

❏ Ex-employees (alumni) can contribute in many ways to your retention efforts.

# Mentoring and Coaching Programs

*If he didn't push you, he didn't like you (referring to his mentor, Charles Tandy).*

> —Bernard Appel
> President, Radio Shack

*When the best leader's work is done, the people say, "We did it ourselves."*

> —Lao-Tzu, philosopher and
> founder of Taoism, *Tao Te Ching*

M any organizations start mentoring, coaching, and/or buddy programs as an important tool to combat excessive or debilitating retention rates among top employees. If you manage top performers, mentoring and coaching are *not optional.* Whether or not your organization has such a formal mentoring or coaching program, your key employees will expect that you provide them with mentoring and coaching when appropriate.

## The Benefits of Mentoring and Coaching Programs

We'll define each type of program (mentoring, coaching, and another—associated—called a "buddy program") in just a moment. But first we should outline the benefits to your key employees of such programs, using a mentoring program as an example.

These programs can help increase retention in three ways:

Among the mentors: If you appoint top employees as mentors, they may stay longer with the organization for one or more of the following reasons:

- They have a stronger sense of personal and career development.
- They experience a greater sense of satisfaction and fulfillment.
- Their sense of responsibility is heightened.
- They feel a desire to complete what they've begun and to remain with strong mentoring relationships that have formed.
- They feel a greater sense of bonding with the organization as the mentors see their efforts make a positive effect in the lives and careers of other employees.
- The mentors feel a sense of responsibility and commitment to their protégés.

**Key Term** **Protégé** A person who is being mentored or coached. Also known as *mentoree*" and *mentee*. If none of these terms excites you, you can just stick with "employee" or "program participant" (if you have a formal mentoring or coaching program). Alternatively, you can coin your own phrase. One of my recent clients came up with the word "mentégé" to describe the mentored participants in her program.

Among the protégés: Employees who are being well mentored may stay longer with the organization for one or more of the following reasons:

- The protégés have a stronger sense of personal and career development.
- The protégés' assessment of the organization

as an employer will be higher because it has the mentoring program.

- The motivational and role-modeling aspects of the mentoring relationship maintain a positive attitude in the protégés.
- The protégés have a forum for discussing and resolving frustrations that might otherwise accumulate to cause the protégés to leave the organization.
- The protégés may view the mentoring program as a fast track to promotion.
- The protégés may fear losing a good mentoring relationship, which may not be available elsewhere.

Among other employees: Those of your employees who are not being mentored will often still be positively impacted, for any of the following reasons:

- Employees in general will perceive the mentoring program as an indication of the organization's commitment to its employees.
- The positive impact on the attitudes and personal and career development of those involved in the program leads to improved employee morale and positive attitude about the organization.
- The mentors' and protégés' managers will see an improvement in the personal and career development of both parties.
- Employees who are not part of the program but will be considered as mentors or protégés in the future may see that opportunity as a further reason to stay with the organization.

**Communication Required!**
Note that these benefits will accrue only if you "sell" the program positively to your employees—not just those being mentored—and if the program is seen as successful. On the other hand, if your employees see the mentoring program as an elitist activity, available for only the few, or if the program is generally considered to be weak or unsuccessful, then the impact on morale may well be negative.

OK, now that we've outlined the benefits of mentoring (and, by extension, coaching and buddy programs), in the rest of this chapter we'll consider the characteristics of each type of program and the differences among them.

## Definitions and Vocabulary

Although the art and science of mentoring and coaching have been developing over many centuries (or perhaps because of it), neither area has a formally accepted vocabulary. Indeed, so loose and varied are the definitions of "mentoring" and "coaching" that the two activities are constantly confused. In particular, the terminology surrounding mentoring has been subject to various uses.

Over the last 10 years or so, the business community has become obsessed with the concept of *leadership*—what it means, how it's practiced, and how to be better at it. Included in that obsessive analysis is a growing fascination with the topic of mentoring. There are many reasons for this—the elusive idea of somehow "duplicating" success (mentoring as cloning), a preoccupation with successful people and their habits (mentoring as lifestyle), and the theory of management as a science (mentoring as an experiment).

There has been an accompanying rapid growth in the number of organizations using mentoring as a managerial, cultural, or development tool. Most of these organizations have designed mentoring programs, using their own vocabulary and definitions of mentoring. As a result, there are hundreds of differing definitions of the terms and phrases used in association with mentoring—not least the definition of "mentoring" itself.

The terms "mentoring" and "coaching" are sometimes used interchangeably; at other times great distinctions are made between the two. One organization's or one manager's definition of *coaching* may exactly match another's definition of *mentoring* and what's known as *mentoring* in Company A will be known as *coaching* in Company B.

In this chapter we will clearly distinguish between mentoring and coaching, using the most commonly accepted definition of each—but these definitions are not universal.

Many individuals and organizations have tried to produce a generally acceptable glossary of mentoring terms and their meanings, with limited success. The definitions of mentoring and coaching produced by professional bodies vary widely ... and even are frequently in contradiction. This lack of formalized definitions is reflected in books and articles. Almost every one of the hundreds or thousands of books on leadership contains at least a passing reference to mentoring. Almost every book defines mentoring differently. Is it passive? Is it active? Is it interventionist? Is it inwardly directed? Is it job-related? Or is it all of the above? Very few of the books you will read on the topic agree on even the most fundamental definitions.

Fortunately, it's not important whether your definitions of the roles and functions in your program match any specific external vocabulary. If you and everyone else in your organization agree on what you mean by terms such as "mentor," "coach," "mentoring," and "coaching," that's all that matters.

Of course, in reaching

> **More Communication Required!**
>
> Without consistent communication, the lack of clear definitions breeds confusion. You can be certain that, right now, your colleagues (and your employees) all have a different concept of mentoring and coaching and what a mentoring or coaching program might be. So, it's of fundamental importance that you clearly define and agree on your terms before introducing formal or informal mentoring or coaching—and that you communicate and use one consistent set of definitions.

internal agreement on definitions, it will be useful for you to you to know what terms other organizations are using as definitions. This knowledge will also help you benchmark with your peers in other organizations and share experiences with them. As you work through this chapter, you'll have an opportunity to compare your own definitions with those used by others. Just don't expect our Key Term sidebars to do all the work for you!

## What Is Mentoring?

### Historical Background

In *The Odyssey*, Mentor was the person entrusted by Odysseus to teach and raise his son Telemachus while he was absent on his many travels. Trustworthy and credible, Mentor soon became the epitome of wise counsel and sage instruction.

Some form of mentoring has always taken place in the business environment, however informally. The friendly discussion over coffee, a few well-chosen words in the rest room after a hasty outburst, and the quiet hand-written note to congratulate a colleague on handling a difficulty well: such activities have always played their part in the development of top employees.

For decades many world-class companies (some famous, like GE, but most unknown outside their own communities) have had more formalized mentoring relationships.

As a manager of key employees you will need to provide at least informal mentoring-based guidance and, depending on the organization, you may well be involved in a more formal mentoring program at some time.

### Defining Terms for Your Mentoring Program

Mentoring is all about people—the people who do the mentoring, the people who are being mentored, and the people who are impacted by the mentoring relationship.

We're going to define the roles and functions in your mentoring program primarily in terms of what people *do*. Designing an effective mentoring program really means putting in place the culture, resources, and structure necessary for two or more people to develop an effective relationship, which will help at least one of them develop.

The first step in designing your mentoring program is to understand who will be involved and what is expected of them. The rest of this chapter will introduce you to the major categories of individuals involved in a mentoring program and give you the opportunity to define for yourself the role they will play in your mentoring program.

## What Is a Mentor?

In the business environment, the role of the mentor has changed over the last five to 10 years.

Until about 10 years ago, a mentor was almost universally seen as an older, senior person who would help someone more junior in whatever manner seemed right to the mentor at the time. There was a sense of quirkiness, capriciousness, about what mentors did.

It was almost as if the decision to act as a mentor was so benevolent that no one had any right to question the mentor about how he (it was almost always he) did it, let alone expect anything structured or accountable. A person was lucky just to have a mentor, so that meant putting up with strange habits or unrealistic expectations and being thankful.

Nowadays, mentoring is a much more accepted part of general business practice and, as with any practice that gets assimilated into the mainstream, mentoring has become less mysterious and more accessible.

Mentors are now much more accountable. There's more agreement on what's expected from the manager as a mentor, what works and what doesn't, and how the mentoring relationship should be structured for optimum results. Today, the role of the mentoring manager is less power-related: it's less about seniority and teaching and more about sharing and development.

In its purest sense, mentoring is about supporting and developing the all-round growth of the protégé, not just helping him or her do the job better.

Here are some statements used by organizations to describe mentors:

- A mentor is someone who supports another individual and is concerned with his or her growth.
- A mentor is concerned for the individual as a person, not just as an employee.
- A mentor is concerned for his protégé's development as a whole, and not just in the job he does.

- A mentor has an independent relationship with her protégé, not one based on authority or power. She will listen, question, and only then advise. Her advice will be given without judgment or criticism of the other as an individual.
- A mentor is above all person-focused. A mentor will have no stake in the relationship, other than wanting to see the development of the individual, and will start with a bias in the protégé's favor.
- A mentor is a trusted friend, a teacher, a guide and role model. He has knowledge that he is prepared to transfer to others, is expert, or at least has advanced status in his field, and is acknowledged as such by his peers.
- A mentor is nurturing by nature, noncompetitive and supportive. She is patient, but prepared to challenge her protégé, shows enthusiasm while maintaining perspective, stays focused while being aspirational.
- A mentor upholds the virtues of his chosen employment, trade, or profession and is loyal to his company or organization, while at the same time recognizing its weaknesses, and constructively helps his protégé deal with those same weaknesses.

As you can see, the composite of the ideal mentor is somewhat daunting—and probably impossible to find. Few individuals would satisfy all of the expectations listed above—but then, the statements came from six organizations. You'll be relieved to know that perfection is not a prerequisite for being a mentor!

The key is to clearly identify the attributes your organization requires in a mentor—which may or may not be similar to those above.

## The Distinction Between a Coach and a Mentor

The distinction between coach and mentor is not always clear-cut. There's ambiguity in all management activities, and the difference between mentoring and coaching can sometimes be elusive.

Below are three checklists of phrases that are positioned along a continuum between coaching and mentoring. The phrases and their position along the continuum will vary from organization to organization. Use the lists to form your own opinion as to what a mentor or a coach will do in your organization. Remember: it's your internal definition that counts, nothing else.

List 1 places some of the words we used to describe a protégé on a continuum between being *coached* and being *mentored*.

| COACH ↑ | | | COACH ↑ | | |
|---|---|---|---|---|---|
| | BEGINNING | ❑ | | QUALIFIED | ❑ |
| | UNQUALIFIED | ❑ | | DISPASSIONATE | ❑ |
| | NEW | ❑ | | CRITICAL | ❑ |
| | JUNIOR | ❑ | | AUTHORITATIVE | ❑ |
| | INEXPERIENCED | ❑ | | INDEPENDENT | ❑ |
| | TEACHABLE | ❑ | | FIRM | ❑ |
| | PROMISING | ❑ | | CHALLENGING | ❑ |
| | LEARNER | ❑ | | TEACHER | ❑ |
| | ENTHUSIASTIC | ❑ | | EXPERIENCED | ❑ |
| | EFFECTIVE | ❑ | | INVOLVED | ❑ |
| | RELECTIVE | ❑ | | SUPPORTIVE | ❑ |
| | INVOLVED | ❑ | | NON-COMPETITIVE | ❑ |
| | GROWING | ❑ | | ASPIRATIONAL | ❑ |
| | QUESTIONING | ❑ | | NON-JUDGMENTAL | ❑ |
| | ASPIRATIONAL | ❑ | | NURTURING | ❑ |
| **MENTOR** ↓ | | | **MENTOR** ↓ | | |

Figure 11-1. Continuum for describing a protégé of a coach or a mentor

Figure 11-2. Continuum for describing a coach or a mentor

List 2 places some of the words we used to describe a coach or a mentor on the same continuum.

Finally, List 3 places phrases regularly used to describe what a mentor does on the same continuum.

The lists can cause some debate, particularly when reviewed

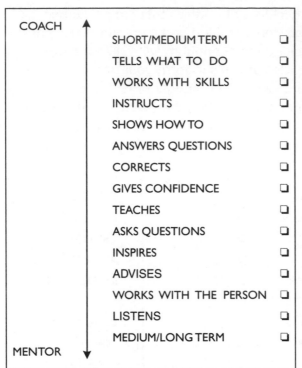

by those who are active coaches or mentors!

These are *generalizations*, nothing engraved in stone; as mentioned earlier, the phrases and their position along the continuum will vary from organization to organization. They're included here to help guide you as you define the role(s) of mentor and/or coach in your specific context.

Figure 11-3. Spreading information over more than one slide

## How Does a Mentor Differ from a Supervisor?

We've already looked at how mentoring and coaching have a different emphasis, with mentors primarily more involved with the *person* and the coach more concerned with the *job*. Continuing this comparison, an individual's supervisor can be said to be more directly concerned about *results*.

- The mentor helps an individual become *more capable*.
- The coach helps an individual become *more competent*.
- The supervisor ensures that an individual *contributes*.

There is also an element of *time-frame differentiation*:

- The supervisor *tells*. The supervisor is primarily concerned about the short term: "Why haven't you produced this output now?"

- The coach *shows*. The coach is more concerned with the medium term: "Here's how to do this right and how to improve in the future."
- The mentor *asks*. The mentor is more concerned with the long-term development of the individual: "What we can learn from this? How would you respond to this differently in the future?"

Another key difference between the role of a mentor and the role of a supervisor is that of *authority*. A mentor will have no direct authority over the protégé, who is free to take advice as he or she wishes, to act or not to act in the light of what he or she hears. A supervisor, on the other hand, will almost always have direct authority over the employee, who will risk punishment if he or she chooses not to do what the supervisor says.

A third essential difference is the *nature of the communication* between supervisor and employee and between mentor and protégé. Although the term "instruction" is often used in both circumstances, it's more correct to say that the supervisor *directs* or *commands* the individual, while the mentor *advises*.

This distinction between *advice* and *direction* is one of the reasons it's so important that mentors (in "pure" mentoring) are not the line managers or supervisors of their protégés. Having the same person play both roles will almost certainly cause the relationship to break down eventually.

## What Is the Difference Between Mentoring and Managing?

Let's bring all this theory down to what you do every day. Isn't every good manager a mentor also? Is it really necessary to differentiate between mentoring and managing?

I would suggest the answer is "Yes." It's essential to distinguish between mentoring as a *management tool* and a *mentoring relationship*. The difference between the two is *independence*: it's not truly possible to have a mentoring relationship with someone who also has direct responsibility for you.

At its core, mentoring is a relationship of openness, freedom, and confidence. The protégé should be free to discuss or not discuss issues as he or she wishes and free to accept or reject the mentor's advice. This is very difficult to do when the mentor is also your direct boss.

Similarly, the mentor must be able to communicate with the protégé without raising concerns regarding potential punishment or reward. If the protégé feels he or she is being assessed for promotion or recognition through the mentoring process, the relationship will never develop into the two-way communication process it should be.

Does this mean that as a manager you cannot be a mentor and shouldn't use mentoring as part of your management style? Of course not. Good managers know the power of mentoring and show mentoring attributes regularly—attributes such as supportiveness, encouragement, and knowledge transfer.

However, it's one thing for occasional mentoring to take place within the management function (mentoring as a management tool) and quite another for a formal mentoring relationship to be established, grow, and flourish. For a protégé to regularly receive the full benefit of the mentoring relationship (and certainly within a formal program environment), the mentor must be someone with whom he or she can be wholly relaxed, outside of the management process.

## Separating Mentoring and Managing

Therefore, for your mentoring program to produce best results, the mentor should not have direct authority over the protégé. What can you do if this isn't possible, if the sheer reality of the numbers means you can't avoid mentoring some of your key employees yourself or appointing an employee's manager or supervisor to serve as his or her mentor, despite your desire to keep the mentoring role "pure"? Here are a few suggestions.

- Consider a many-to-one mentoring program, where one mentor has more than one protégé.

- Consider "jumping" one reporting layer up. Can you make the supervisor's supervisor the mentor? Could your manager act as the mentor of some of your key employees?
- If going up a level would put a strain on the numbers (as there will be fewer possible mentors at the higher level), then consider a many-to-one mentoring program at that level.
- Pair with another company in a similar business but with which you don't compete, to swap mentors. Your local Chamber of Commerce or similar organization can help you find possible partners.
- Bring back retired employees to assist with the mentoring program. They'll love to be asked—and it certainly won't hurt your community profile.
- If the program is for new hires or junior managers, consider appointing "high flyer" peers as mentors. This situation needs to be handled carefully to avoid causing friction, but where the "high flyers" are already well recognized, it can work.
- Do you have multiple locations, but with limited numbers at each location? If supervisors and managers from one location make regular visits to another, try speaking to one of them and "doing a deal" whereby he or she mentors some of your key employees while visiting and you can mentor some of his or her employees. Between visits, the mentors and their protégés can keep in contact by e-mail and other methods.
- Consider "employees" with subcontract status. Some of your best people are not technically employed by you, but may make excellent mentors. Look particularly at those who either have been subcontractors to you for a long time (and therefore know your business well) or were once on the payroll before going independent.
- Think about your supply chain. You or others in your organization probably know some excellent potential

mentors working in your favorite customer and supplier companies. Many of these folks will have worked with your organization and will know it intimately. Your marketing or purchasing manager can help identify suitable companies and may be thrilled to get the opportunity to deepen the bond between the two organizations.

## How Does a Coach Differ from a Mentor?

The role of a coach is less focused on the *individual* and more focused on the *job* than the role of the mentor. A coach helps the protégé do his or her job better. Although some of the elements of the mentoring role may be present—such as motivation, performance enhancement, awareness, transfer of skills, and effectiveness—the coach's primary concern is not the growth of the individual, but rather the better performance of the job. The coach can be seen as exerting an influence, in being directive in trying to achieve his or her goals; a coach will frequently say, "Here, do it like this...." A mentor, if talking about an operational issue (which is less likely), is more inclined to ask, "Have you thought about trying...?" or "What other ways have you thought of doing this...?"

It's easier for you to coach a direct employee than to mentor him or her. Unlike the "purist" mentoring of the previous section, a coach can also be the individual's manager or supervisor, although that's not necessary. Coaching is more directive and job-related and less related to personal growth than mentoring, which allows some overlap between the roles of coach and manager (or supervisor) that's not possible for the mentor.

Coaching is also more closely aligned with on-the-job training than is mentoring. A coach will often follow up after on-the-job training and help the employee translate classroom training into practice or better his or her practical skills.

Coaching is also frequently linked with formal qualifications. If you have an employee who is studying for professional qualifications, you or someone else may well coach him or her to develop book skills into both practical application and success on examinations. In contrast, a mentor is unlikely to get involved in on-the-job or skills-related training—unless, for example, a persistent inability to progress in this area is causing a personal or career development issue for the protégé.

## Two More Possibilities

In a chapter devoted to mentoring and coaching, it seems appropriate to discuss, at least briefly, two related types of assistance, the "buddy" program and executive coaching.

### "Buddy" Program

A relatively recent development in the "mentoring" arena is the growth of so-called "buddy" programs.

I've put "mentoring" in quotes because buddy programs aren't really mentoring in its purest sense, in that the buddy relationship involves no or very little personal or career development. A buddy program is most frequently designed for new hires: a new employee is matched with another employee, often someone with only a few months' more experience than the new arrival.

A "buddy" may do no more than show the new employee the ropes—how things work in the organization, where to go to get supplies, how to submit forms or report an accident, and so on. Sometimes the relationship involves some low-level supervision. Most buddy relationships include some "unofficial mentoring" in that the experienced employee will share political information—who's in,

> **Key Term**
>
> **Buddy program** A program in which each new hire is assigned a more experienced employee who will provide guidance, especially during the first few months, helping the new employee become acquainted with the policies, procedures, and culture of the organization.
>
> Buddy programs are not to be confused with mentoring programs. The experienced buddy is not usually expected to provide personal or career development for the other, but simply to make it easier for the other employee to become acclimated.

who's out, who best to approach with a certain problem, why certain things are done in certain ways.

The relationship can begin one-way and then, after the initial period, become more two-way, as each "buddy" is looking out for the other, providing shift or other cover, and generally taking responsibility for the other's welfare.

If there are safety issues in your business, for example, you may wish to have a continuing buddy program for all your employees, so they can watch out for each other. The relationship can be two-way from the outset. You may also want to run a "buddy" program as an adjunct to your mentoring program, especially for new hires.

A properly implemented buddy program is simple to construct and manage and it can be a real boon to you as a manager by taking away from the relationship with your key employees much of the less important, time-consuming "trivia" of the daily workload, leaving you to concentrate on higher-level, more strategic communications.

There are circumstances in which everyone needs a buddy—formally or not. The checklist will help you decide if you should incorporate a buddy program into your mentoring activities.

---

### Do You Need a Buddy Program?

Here's a checklist of the circumstances in which you should consider implementing a buddy program.

- Where your new hires (or job changers) need to know how to use equipment or technology, but there's little or no formal on-the-job training.
- Where you do on-the-job training, but a period of assisted practical application is required to convert the training to acquired skills.
- Where access to necessary equipment or technology is restricted and needs to be shared or "hot-desked."
- Where new hires or job changers need to assimilate new policies or vocabulary in a short time.
- Where new hires are clogging up your HR department with routine inquiries.

- Where there are issues such as shift sharing and sick or vacation coverage that can be resolved more effectively by pairing employees than by trying to juggle schedules.
- Where the safety issues in your production line require employees to look out for each other.
- When employees can benefit from having a co-worker involved in their day-to-day activities, such as sales calls and quality inspections.
- In acquisitions, mergers, or reorganizations, where two separate departments are being combined and employees in each need to learn the other's processes.
- Where you work closely with your supply chain partners and they assign some of their employees temporarily to your organization.
- Where you have a long-term consulting program in place and there are term consultants working in your organization for more than three months.
- Where employees transfer for medium-term periods to other locations within your organization.

### Executive Coaching

Another form of coaching is termed "executive coaching." This is where an external consultant is hired to work with an individual executive (usually senior) to assist in his or her development.

Adding to the confusion of terminology, this form of coaching is really more like mentoring, in that it usually deals with the whole of the executive's development and not just job-related skills. (Executive coaching is rarely skill- or job-related.) As the use of external coaches is not within the scope of this book, the distinction need not detain us—but you should be aware of the terminology.

> **Executive coaching** A situation in which an external consultant is hired to work with an executive (usually at the senior level) to help him or her develop. This "coaching" is actually more like mentoring than like coaching.

## Manager's Checklist for Chapter 11

❏ Mentoring and coaching are an essential part of your relationship with key employees.

❑ The terminology of mentoring and coaching is not standardized and can be confusing.

❑ It's important that *you* know what you mean by "mentoring" and "coaching."

❑ It's hard for an employee's manager to also be his or her mentor.

❑ It's quite possible (and usual) for a manager to be an employee's coach.

❑ Buddy programs can help you build higher-quality relationships with your top employees.

# Summary: Making It All Work

*Excellence results from dedication to daily progress.*
*Making something a little bit better every day.*
　　　　　　　　—Robert Hall, Indiana University

*It is commitment, not authority, that produces results.*
　　　　　　　　—William L. Gore, founder and
　　　　　　　　CEO, W.L. Gore & Associates

In this chapter we'll take everything in this book and translate it into a strategy you can easily implement and use to retain your top employees.

The issue of retention is generally stressful for most managers. Managing high performing employees can also be stressful at times. Combine the two and consider the issue of retaining top employees and you have a recipe for mega-stress. In this chapter we'll discuss four ways to reduce the stress involved in retaining top performers while maximizing the applicability of all you've learned so far.

## "Toto, I Have a Feeling We're Not in Kansas Anymore"

The first and most significant way to ease the implementation of the retention strategies detailed in this book is to make sure your own mindset is appropriate. Here's a reminder of two of the mindset adjustments we've already discussed and yet another.

### Remember the New Contract

The relationship between employers and employees has changed. There's no underlying assumption that employees will stay with an organization for all or even a significant part of their working lives.

It's very important to keep this in mind. Many managers believe that their objective is to prevent good employees from leaving the organization. That's unrealistic. There's enough stress involved in retaining top performers without adding unrealistic self-imposed objectives!

### People Leave: Manage It as You Can

A corollary of the new employment contract is that *good people will leave your organization.*
Whatever you may do, top performers will still reach a stage in their careers when they believe it's right for them to move on. Some hiring decisions will turn out to be wrong, causing some employees to leave after only a short time. Sometimes, despite the best intentions, the employer-employee relationship will just not work.

> **MISTAKE PROOFING**
>
> ### Working in a Time Warp?
>
> If senior management of your organization still believes in the old "status quo" employment contract, you've got more stress. You're expected to manage and relate to your top employees in a way that will actually work against effective retention, by assuming a relationship that doesn't exist.
>
> If you're in this position, you can choose either to adopt guerilla tactics (using what you've learned in this book, but keeping below senior management radar so as not to rock the boat) or to try educating your senior managers on this point. A diplomatically placed copy of this book might be a great start!

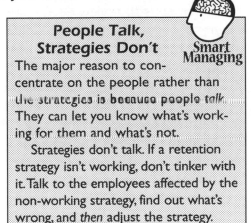

**No Turnover Is Poor Retention**

Even if you reduced your turnover of top employees to zero, you would *still* have a retention problem— maybe an even bigger problem!

That's because every organization needs a steady influx of new blood to keep it vibrant, growing, and responsive to outside changes. A turnover rate of less than about 5% is dangerously low (especially for top performers).

Keeping your organization alive and thriving means *not* managing the turnover of key employees down to a dangerously low level. As long as your turnover rate is not too high (between say 6% and 12%, depending on your industry), you can think of each departing employee as an opportunity to prevent the organization from becoming stagnant.

Again, it's important to approach such "discontinuities" with a relaxed mindset. Don't take it personally and become defensive or, worse, aggressive about departures. That just adds to the stress and does nothing for retention.

Even with the techniques detailed in this book, not every high performer will stay with you forever—so remember to keep the door open to employees who leave.

### Concentrate on People, Not Strategies

Remember that effective retention is about *people*, not *strategies*. When you implement the strategies in this book, focus them on your *people*. What works? What doesn't work? Who's content? Who's discontent-

**People Talk, Strategies Don't**

The major reason to concentrate on the people rather than the strategies is because people *talk*. They can let you know what's working for them and what's not.

Strategies don't talk. If a retention strategy isn't working, don't tinker with it. Talk to the employees affected by the non-working strategy, find out what's wrong, and *then* adjust the strategy.

ed? What's causing the discontent? Address those needs.

## It's All About Adding Value

After making an appropriate change in mindset, the next step in implementing your top employee retention strategy effectively is to ensure that each element *adds value*. That's important in reducing potential stress and friction.

This is particularly so after the "honeymoon period" that all such initiatives go through. At first, senior management is enthusiastic about your retention activities. Then, after some time, someone asks, "What is this actually achieving for us? These hiring practices, this expensive orientation program, the revamped compensation and rewards packages, all this mentoring and coaching—what's it getting for us?"

To answer such questions, you've got to show not only that your retention strategy has reduced turnover of top performers, but also that each element of your retention strategy adds value. In this context, the concept of adding value means that each event, activity, or process in your retention strategy should result in a net gain for the individuals involved and/or for the organization, rather than a net consumption of resources. If any element doesn't add value, then it should be stopped.

## Adding Value for the Organization

The first step is to review each element of your strategy to ensure that at each step there's clear, demonstrable added value for the organization. For example, if you're implementing an orientation program or an "employee of the month" award, in what ways will it help the organization meet its goals?

The answers in many cases will be obvious: the orientation program will ensure that the employees do their jobs better and the "employee of the month" award will raise performance levels. In other cases, it may be harder to identify the value, such as with raising compensation levels, for example, or instituting a non-skills-related mentoring program.

Identify and list the ways in which each retention element adds value at the organizational level. Keep your list handy and add to it as other thoughts occur: at some stage you'll find it essential in defending your retention strategies.

## Adding Value to the Top Employees

It's equally important that your retention strategies add value for the top employees. Otherwise, the program will fall into disuse.

The simplest way to do this is to review your list and add a note about how each element adds value for the employees involved. Again, that will be easier for some elements of your program and less so for other elements. If you fail to find any way in which some element of your retention strategy adds value for your top performers, either alter it to do so or scrap it.

## Adding Value for You

When designing your top employee retention strategy, did you encounter any elements that inconvenience you significantly? If there are elements of your strategy that consume your resources (your time and energy, primarily) and don't deliver an obvious added value for *you*, then chances are that over time your support and enthusiasm for those elements will wane and eventually die.

This is a very common cause of death for retention initiatives: there's little or no personal benefit for the championing manager to continue putting the energy and resources into the activity.

Of course, all retention activities are making your job easier by reducing turnover of top employees, but this benefit is medi-

---

### Make the Added Value Tangible

**TRICKS OF THE TRADE**

Make the ways in which retention activities add value for you as tangible as possible. If you award an "employee of the month," hold the dinner in a restaurant you enjoy visiting. If you institute a mentoring program, make sure you personally mentor someone you enjoy sharing time with.

These suggestions may seem simple, but you're more likely to continue with these activities than if you're making the "employee of the month" award in a corner of the company cafeteria in a rushed lunch hour between meetings or you're involved in mentoring the employee from hell.

Make it work for you and you'll be more committed to making it work for others.

um-term, nebulous, and hard to appreciate amid the pressures of day-to-day operational activities. To remain enthusiastic, you need to be able to see added value in the short term.

### Adding Value for Others

Finally, make sure the entire retention process adds value for everyone else in the organization. Your retention activities will be constricted and eventually die if they fail to add value for those who are involved on the periphery and who have the power of making the process succeed or fail.

If, for example, an orientation program takes up so much of your assistant's time that he's falling behind in his core duties, something needs to be altered—either the program design or your assistant's duties. Similarly, if your skills coaching program is consuming so much of the computer lab time that other managers are complaining, you need to either redesign the coaching program or use different resources.

You might find a chart like the one in Figure 12-1 helpful in establishing the added value of your retention activities.

| Retention Program Element | Added Value to the Organization | Added Value to Top Employees | Added Value to Me | Added Value to Others Involved |
|---|---|---|---|---|
|  |  |  |  |  |
|  |  |  |  |  |
|  |  |  |  |  |
|  |  |  |  |  |

Figure 12-1. Added value chart

## Using Points of Leverage in Your Organization

After making an appropriate change in mindset and ensuring that your retention strategy adds value, the next step is to establish and use four effective points of leverage within the organization:

- A senior management champion
- The senior management team
- The top performer peer group
- Yourself

## A Senior Management Champion

The most essential point of leverage for your retention strategy is a senior management champion—someone at a senior level who is passionately in favor of what you're trying to achieve, understands the issues involved, and is prepared to publicly associate with it.

A senior management champion will specifically be of assistance in the following respects:

- "Selling" your program to the senior management team. Acting as a go-between and an advocate, the champion is your representative at the senior management level, helping you get the approvals and support you require.
- Providing advice. You'll often want to seek guidance from a member of senior management as you design and implement your retention program. Your program champion should be the source of that help.
- Acting as a figurehead for the program. There will be occasions (award ceremonies, program launches, focus groups with your top performers) when the pres-

### How to Find a Program Champion

You might be lucky: you might know who your senior management program champion is or is likely to be. You might even be spectacularly fortunate, if the program champion is your manager or supervisor, since that makes communication and working together much easier.

But what if you cannot readily identify such a champion? Then, your best strategy is to engage with the person from senior management who has the most to gain by your efforts—your manager or whoever benefits most from the activities of your top team. Explain what you're trying to achieve, demonstrate how that person will clearly benefit, and ask for his or her support.

**Smart Managing**

ence of a representative from senior management can be exceptionally motivating. Your champion should be your first choice for such activities.

### The Senior Management Team

Your next most important point of leverage is the senior management team. The more visibly and actively the team supports your retention activities, the more credible the process becomes. For your retention activities to gain acceptance in the organizational culture, you need more than passive support from the management team; you need *proactive engagement* in the process.

**Think Long**
Brief your senior management champion once a month or so and provide everything he or she needs to give the senior management team concise, accurate, and motivational summaries of what's happened in the previous month, with supporting data. Make yourself easily accessible if your champion has any queries. Most important of all, ask for the sale. In your case, this means identifying just one or two straightforward ways in which the senior management team can support your activities in the next month—calling an award winner, sending a memo of congratulations, attending a social event—and asking your champion to ask the other members of senior management to get involved.

### The Top Employee Peer Group

After ensuring the involvement of your senior management team, the next most important point of leverage in the organization is the top employees. Let's face it: if the best performers reject your retention activities, then everything you do will come to naught.

It's essential to involve your top employee team from the outset. There are three cardinal rules to remember: communicate, communicate, and (you guessed it!) communicate.

Make your retention strategy transparent. No one on your top team should need to guess what you're doing. Let them know about your intentions, your goals, and your fears and ask for their support.

**Yourself**

Finally, don't forget the most important point of leverage of all—you. It's your idea. You have the most to gain. Your commitment and enthusiasm will make the difference between success and failure of the entire project.

Before you start implementing your retention strategy, take a long, hard look at its components. Which excite you most? Which interest you only somewhat? And—most important—which are you less than enthusiastic about?

**Watch the Dark Side**

Many managers are great at communicating positive and motivational activities—announcing awards, redesigning compensation, structuring a mentoring program, and so forth. Make sure you also communicate with your high performers about the possible risks involved in your retention activities—that they may demotivate other employees, make reporting systems overly complicated, take up too much senior management time, or whatever. You will find their help and advice on these points invaluable.

Perhaps you've concluded that you need a better orientation program for your new hires, but the prospect of designing and implementing such a program doesn't really grab you. Or perhaps you've realized that your compensation and bonus structure needs to be revised, but the idea of arguing about it with the HR department drains any enthusiasm you might have.

For one reason or another, some aspects of your retention program won't thrill you. Beware! Therein lies the greatest danger to the entire strategy. In the worst scenario, you'll procrastinate about these aspects of your program. That procrastination will turn to neglect and the whole strategy will fail.

It's vital to your success that you tackle the *hardest* parts of your strategy *first*—now, while you're most committed. Don't wait!

## Building a Retention Culture

The final point to remember in implementing your top employee retention strategy is *longevity*. You definitely don't want to have to repeat all of this activity in a year or two. There's little

### Get a Buddy

**Smart Managing**   If there's a danger of procrastinating with implementing elements of your top employee retention strategy, why not get a buddy to keep you on track?

Find a like-minded (or at least sympathetic) peer who is interested in developing a similar strategy for his or her top employees or at least supportive of your strategy. Ask that person to be your buddy—someone who will knock on your door to find out how you're doing, prod you to stay on schedule, and remind you of your reasons for doing this and the benefits.

If you're really lucky, you might find that your buddy has complementary skills and interests. Maybe he or she will take on that orientation program design or help you think through ways to approach the HR department!

more dispiriting than designing and implementing a retention strategy and seeing it succeed, only to find that you have to do the whole thing all over again as employees get promoted, transfer internally, or, eventually, leave the organization. (Remember: even the best retention strategy won't make anyone stay forever.)

This means designing and implementing your strategy in such a way that it will continue to operate over time with minimum maintenance.

### You Shouldn't Have to Push Water Uphill

The first way to recognize that you may have longevity problems with a specific part of your retention strategy is the ease with which it can be introduced. If you're finding it difficult to get people to accept and participate in some part of your program, then it's highly likely that this part will fall into disuse over time.

The key in such circumstances is to find the *root cause* of the resistance and to deal with that. If, for example, you design a social events calendar to promote teamwork and assimilation, but find that employees aren't signing up for it, ask some questions. Is it because everyone is already working too hard to want to spend any leisure time together? Is it because the events you've proposed are not very exciting? Is it because the same idea was tried a few years ago and was an embarrassing failure? Identify the root cause and deal with it before proceeding with implementation.

> **Pilot Your Activities**    MISTAKE PROOFING
>
> One great way to find out the ease of implementing any part of your strategy—with minimum disruption and without risking that the entire strategy will be labeled a failure—is to *pilot* the activity first. To test a social events calendar, for example, try just a few events with a few people. If that works well enough, then roll out the entire calendar.

### Processes vs. Events

Second, try to put in place *processes,* not just *events.* This means designing not just each specific element of your retention strategy, but also the supporting structure to ensure that the event can be repeated without the need for your intervention.

For example, let's say you decide to implement a mentoring program for your top employees. You'll engage in a series of events: setting the program objectives, identifying protégés and mentors, matching them, getting them launched on their relationship, and monitoring their progress. Make each step a process. For example, write a simple memo detailing your method for matching protégés and mentors, to save someone time and effort the next time around, and file the forms and documents you use to track the mentoring relationships, for future use.

At each step, ask yourself, "If I weren't here tomorrow, is there enough documentation that anyone else could readily step in and manage this strategy?" If the answer is "No," then you're probably implementing events rather than processes and the longevity of your strategy is at risk.

### Warp and Woof

Third, to ensure longevity of your retention strategy, try to make it as much as possible part of the "warp and woof" of the organization. The more your strategy sticks out as something distinct and separate, the more difficult it is to sustain it over time. On the other hand, the more your retention activities are just "what we do here," the more they will be sustained by day-to-day operations.

Here are a few examples:

- Include a "retention effect" assessment of compensation as part of the normal, annual, or periodic compensation review process.
- Make the social calendar part of the regular responsibility of someone who *already* plans events—the press department (if you have one), the CEO's assistant, or whoever plans training or other functions.
- Make the availability of mentoring or coaching an inherent part of the standard performance review process.

The more your retention strategy becomes part of the culture and the less it stands out as something "other," the better!

### Peer Group Maintenance

Finally, as with all good systems, the best retention process is self-sustaining and self-maintaining.

Regularly seek advice and assistance from your top performers. How can *they* help maintain the strategy? What processes can they put in place? In what ways can they help assimilate the program into the warp and woof of the organization? How can they contribute to the program's longevity?

> **Smart Managing**
> ### Transfer Ownership
> The ideas that your top performers will offer will probably include those already suggested above. But this is about more than ideas. If the ideas come from your employees, they're taking ownership of those ideas. That process is much more likely to lead to sustained implementation than if the ideas came from you, generated and imposed from above.

## And Finally...

You've reached the end of what I trust was a rewarding and thought-provoking journey through the mind of your top employees and what you can best do to retain them. I'm assuming you've highlighted the parts of greatest interest, turned down page corners, and made notes.

Now it's time to go back to the start, read through those parts once more, and draw together ideas to form your strategy for retaining your top performers.

Make sure it works for you. Make sure it looks like fun.

I wish you the very best in your endeavors!

## Manager's Checklist for Chapter 12

❏ Successful retention strategies start with the right mindset.

❏ Retention strategies can induce stress. The best way to minimize the stress is to have an appropriate mindset.

❏ Make sure your strategy adds value throughout the organization.

❏ Use all the points of leverage you can find.

❏ Get senior management involved.

❏ Implement *processes*, not *events*.

❏ Above all, stay enthusiastic!

# Index

## About the Author

**J. Leslie McKeown** is the President and CEO of Deliver The Promise® and has over 20 years' experience in working with organizations in Europe, the U.S., and Asia.

Les qualified as a Chartered Accountant in the UK in 1978. Four years later, he started his own consulting practice, building a lifelong career in advising individuals and companies on growth and development. When he sold his share in the practice to his business partner in 1998, it had grown to a 13-office worldwide training and consulting business.

Les now lives in Tiburon, California, where he trains, speaks, and writes on the recruitment, retention, and development of high-caliber employees. Les has worked with such organizations as United Technologies (UTC), Xerox, Overture (formerly Goto.com), British Aerospace, Microsoft, Guardian Life, and Kaiser Permanente.

Les can be contacted by mail at Deliver The Promise®, P.O. Box 954, Tiburon, CA 94920, USA, by phone at (415) 789-5014, by e-mail at les@deliverthepromise.com, or through his Web site: **www.deliverthepromise.com**.